OPPOSING VIEWPOINTS® SERIES

Teen Drug Abuse

Other Books of Related Interest:

Opposing Viewpoints Series

Drug Abuse

Gateway Drugs

The War on Drugs

At Issue Series

Club Drugs

Does Advertising Promote Substance Abuse?

Performance Enhancing Drugs

Current Controversies Series

Drug Legalization

Prescription Drugs

"Congress shall make no law . . . abridging the freedom of speech, or of the press."

First Amendment to the U.S. Constitution

The basic foundation of our democracy is the First Amendment guarantee of freedom of expression. The Opposing Viewpoints Series is dedicated to the concept of this basic freedom and the idea that it is more important to practice it than to enshrine it.

OPPOSING VIEWPOINTS® SERIES

| Teen Drug Abuse

David E. Nelson, book editor

GREENHAVEN PRESS
A part of Gale, Cengage Learning

GALE
CENGAGE Learning·

Detroit • New York • San Francisco • New Haven, Conn • Waterville, Maine • London

Christine Nasso, *Publisher*
Elizabeth Des Chenes, *Managing Editor*

© 2011 Greenhaven Press, a part of Gale, Cengage Learning.

Gale and Greenhaven Press are registered trademarks used herein under license.

For more information, contact:
Greenhaven Press
27500 Drake Rd.
Farmington Hills, MI 48331-3535
Or you can visit our Internet site at gale.cengage.com

For product information and technology assistance, contact us at

Gale Customer Support, 1-800-877-4253
For permission to use material from this text or product, submit all requests online at www.cengage.com/permissions

Further permissions questions can be e-mailed to permissionrequest@cengage.com

Articles in Greenhaven Press anthologies are often edited for length to meet page requirements. In addition, original titles of these works are changed to clearly present the main thesis and to explicitly indicate the author's opinion. Every effort is made to ensure that Greenhaven Press accurately reflects the original intent of the authors. Every effort has been made to trace the owners of copyrighted material.

Cover Image copyright © iStockPhoto.com/Ian McDonnell.

LIBRARY OF CONGRESS CATALOGING-IN-PUBLICATION DATA

Teen drug abuse / David E. Nelson, book editor.
      p. cm. -- (Opposing viewpoints)
   Includes bibliographical references and index.
   ISBN 978-0-7377-4992-2 (hardcover) -- ISBN 978-0-7377-4993-9 (pbk.)
   1. Teenagers--Drug use--Juvenile literature. 2. Drug abuse--Prevention--Juvenile literature. 3. Youth--Alcohol use--Juvenile literature. I. Nelson, David Erik.
   HV5824.Y68T43 2010
   362.290835--dc22
                                                          2010018884

Contents

Chapter 3: What Are the Causes and Effects of Teen Substance Abuse?

Chapter 4: How Can Teen Drug Abuse Be Prevented?

Why Consider Opposing Viewpoints?

> *"The only way in which a human being can make some approach to knowing the whole of a subject is by hearing what can be said about it by persons of every variety of opinion and studying all modes in which it can be looked at by every character of mind. No wise man ever acquired his wisdom in any mode but this."*
>
> John Stuart Mill

In our media-intensive culture it is not difficult to find differing opinions. Thousands of newspapers and magazines and dozens of radio and television talk shows resound with differing points of view. The difficulty lies in deciding which opinion to agree with and which "experts" seem the most credible. The more inundated we become with differing opinions and claims, the more essential it is to hone critical reading and thinking skills to evaluate these ideas. Opposing Viewpoints books address this problem directly by presenting stimulating debates that can be used to enhance and teach these skills. The varied opinions contained in each book examine many different aspects of a single issue. While examining these conveniently edited opposing views, readers can develop critical thinking skills such as the ability to compare and contrast authors' credibility, facts, argumentation styles, use of persuasive techniques, and other stylistic tools. In short, the Opposing Viewpoints Series is an ideal way to attain the higher-level thinking and reading skills so essential in a culture of diverse and contradictory opinions.

In addition to providing a tool for critical thinking, Opposing Viewpoints books challenge readers to question their own strongly held opinions and assumptions. Most people form their opinions on the basis of upbringing, peer pressure, and personal, cultural, or professional bias. By reading carefully balanced opposing views, readers must directly confront new ideas as well as the opinions of those with whom they disagree. This is not to simplistically argue that everyone who reads opposing views will—or should—change his or her opinion. Instead, the series enhances readers' understanding of their own views by encouraging confrontation with opposing ideas. Careful examination of others' views can lead to the readers' understanding of the logical inconsistencies in their own opinions, perspective on why they hold an opinion, and the consideration of the possibility that their opinion requires further evaluation.

Evaluating Other Opinions

To ensure that this type of examination occurs, Opposing Viewpoints books present all types of opinions. Prominent spokespeople on different sides of each issue as well as well-known professionals from many disciplines challenge the reader. An additional goal of the series is to provide a forum for other, less known, or even unpopular viewpoints. The opinion of an ordinary person who has had to make the decision to cut off life support from a terminally ill relative, for example, may be just as valuable and provide just as much insight as a medical ethicist's professional opinion. The editors have two additional purposes in including these less known views. One, the editors encourage readers to respect others' opinions—even when not enhanced by professional credibility. It is only by reading or listening to and objectively evaluating others' ideas that one can determine whether they are worthy of consideration. Two, the inclusion of such viewpoints encourages the important critical thinking skill of objectively evaluating an author's credentials and bias. This evaluation will illuminate an author's reasons for taking a particular stance on an issue and will aid in readers' evaluation of the author's ideas.

It is our hope that these books will give readers a deeper understanding of the issues debated and an appreciation of the complexity of even seemingly simple issues when good and honest people disagree. This awareness is particularly important in a democratic society such as ours in which people enter into public debate to determine the common good. Those with whom one disagrees should not be regarded as enemies but rather as people whose views deserve careful examination and may shed light on one's own.

Thomas Jefferson once said that "difference of opinion leads to inquiry, and inquiry to truth." Jefferson, a broadly educated man, argued that "if a nation expects to be ignorant and free . . . it expects what never was and never will be." As individuals and as a nation, it is imperative that we consider the opinions of others and examine them with skill and discernment. The Opposing Viewpoints Series is intended to help readers achieve this goal.

David L. Bender and Bruno Leone,
Founders

Introduction

"The degree to which teens disapprove of use of the drug [marijuana] has recently begun to decline. Changes in these beliefs and attitudes are often very influential in driving changes in use."

—Lloyd Johnston,
principal investigator,
University of Michigan
Monitoring the Future program

There can be no doubt that a substantial portion of American teens uses drugs. According to the University of Michigan's well-regarded Monitoring the Future project (which has annually measured adolescent drug use since 1975), roughly 40 percent of today's high school seniors have used drugs in the past year—which is actually an improvement.

In the late 1970s and early 1980s more than half of all high school seniors reported having used illicit drugs in the previous twelve months. A decade later—amid a flurry of anti-drug messages from the federal government, schools, youth organizations, parents, and peers—that percentage had been halved: barely 25 percent of high school seniors had tried drugs. But, over the next half-decade the portion of teens experimenting with illicit substances increased sharply, steadily climbing to 40 percent, where it has hovered for almost two decades.

In that same five year period during which annual teen drug use quickly climbed from its low of 25 percent to the current 40 percent, the number of teens in drug rehabilitation programs rose by about 42 percent, with the number of teens forced into such programs by courts or schools up almost 50 percent. Meanwhile, the number of teen rehabilitation programs in the United States drastically increased, blossoming into what is now a billion-dollar industry of predominantly privately run programs operated with little government oversight or regulation. While it's tempting to see this as simple cause and effect—more teens turned to drugs, and so more adults took action to help them—it is curious that society cut teen drug use in half before the advent and popularization of such drug rehab programs, but has only been able to hold drug use steady since, even with a whole new arsenal of psychotherapeutic, social, and pharmacological treatments.

Teen alcohol use has showed a slightly different trend: While more than 70 percent of high school seniors drank monthly in 1980, by the early '90s this number had dipped to just below 50 percent, and despite a slight increase through the mid-1990s, it has since sunk to just over 40 percent. Cultural changes can account for the initial 20-percentage-point decrease: Mothers Against Drunk Driving formed in 1980, followed by Students Against Drunk Driving in 1981; both were highly influential in raising awareness of the many fatalities attributable to underage drinking, and did much to change adolescent attitudes toward alcohol. Additionally, the National Minimum Drinking Age Act went into law in 1984, implicitly raising the drinking age nationwide to twenty-one (individual states had previously set drinking ages at their own discretion, with some as low as eighteen). This change sharply limited teen access to alcohol. Although these measures seem to have had a great impact, contributing to that initial, steady decline in alcohol use, no special measures or national initiatives have been implemented since the mid-1990s, even as teen drinking rates have continued to gently decline and teen disapproval of drinking has continued to increase.

The data seems to indicate that the culture can powerfully shift teen substance use patterns, although we have little clear notion of what tactics are responsible for which results. Why did slightly limiting access to alcohol in 1984 have such a profound and lasting effect on teen drinking, while a complete prohibition on most drugs seems to have no impact on their popularity with teens at all? Why do MADD and SADD continue to successfully ward high schoolers away from alcohol, even as DARE and "Just Say NO!" have lost their impact? Increasingly, researchers are coming to agree with the Monitoring the Future program's principal investigator, Lloyd Johnston, who indicates that the primary driving force behind changes in adolescent substance abuse are a teen's perception of the risk and acceptability of using drugs—or, more importantly, that teens assessment of his or her peers' entrenched attitudes toward drugs. Unfortunately, finding a way to reliably guide these group attitudes, and change them in a lasting way, has proved frustratingly difficult.

The contributors to *Opposing Viewpoints: Teen Drug Abuse* examine the many dimensions of substance use and abuse among teens. They explore these in four chapters: How Serious Is Teen Drug Abuse? Does Alcohol Pose a Special Threat to Teens? What Are the Causes and Effects of Teen Substance Abuse? How Can Teen Drug Abuse Be Prevented? Despite the enormous number of teen drug stories and daily tragedies recounted in the daily news and television dramas, there is little consensus as to the extent of America's adolescent drug problem, what its long-term repercussions might be, and how it can be productively addressed.

OPPOSING
VIEWPOINTS®
SERIES

CHAPTER 1

How Serious Is Teen Drug Abuse?

Chapter Preface

It is difficult to meaningfully gauge how serious a problem teen drug abuse is in the United States. This statement likely seems absurd: Turn on the television and new and dangerous teen drug and alcohol trends are exposed weekly, if not nightly—with terrifying anti-drug ads from the Montana Meth Project at every commercial break; newspapers and Web sites likewise serve up tales of teens huffing spray-cleaners and attending parties where they randomly pop pills pilfered from home. Television dramas like *CSI, Boston Legal, Law & Order, Saving Grace,* and *The Wire* highlight the ever more extreme and degrading escapades of drug-bingeing adolescents.

Despite the media hysteria, it is actually very difficult to reliably pinpoint any verifiable teen drug mania. For almost 35 years the University of Michigan has conducted its annual Monitoring the Future survey, which tracks adolescent drug use patterns and attitudes. When the project began in 1975, it surveyed only twelfth graders; it has since expanded, and now surveys 50,000 eighth, tenth, and twelfth graders each year, compiling their responses into a report that is released to the public, as is the data it is based on.

Monitoring the Future reports that teen drug use has stayed steady, or shown a gradual—but definite—decline for almost two decades. This includes cigarette smoking, which has shown a pronounced decline over the course of the study, becoming much less common and much less acceptable among teens. This directly contradicts most Americans' impression of teen drug use. Consider the "Meth Epidemic" of the mid-2000s. This explosion in the popularity of home-cooked speed—especially among teens—was deemed so severe that Congress dedicated a subsection of the anti-terrorism PATRIOT Act to curbing methamphetamine production. One provision of the "U.S. Combat Methamphetamine Epidemic

Act of 2005" strictly limited access to common over-the-counter cold medicine, often requiring cold, flu, and allergy sufferers to show identification and sign an affidavit before purchasing what was once regarded as an innocuous decongestant with no abuse potential. Nonetheless, even as lawmakers were drafting this legislation, Monitoring the Future indicated that methamphetamine use (both among adults and teens) had actually been steadily declining for more than a decade.

Although this highly respected study is theoretically the basis of much U.S. drug policy, the degree to which it influences actual policy—or can do so in the face of terrifying news stories of teen "pharm" parties and sex-for-meth drug cartels—is doubtful. The authors of the following viewpoints explore the breadth and depth of teen drug abuse, in the hopes of clarifying this vital, but distressingly murky, issue.

| "For our purposes, the kinds of self-medicating our teens are doing is less important than the fact that they feel they have to self-medicate at all."

All Teen Drug and Alcohol Use Is Abuse

Mike Linderman and Gary Brozek

Mike Linderman is a Gulf War veteran and licensed counselor who has worked with troubled teens for more than a decade. The following viewpoint is drawn from his book The Teen Whisperer: How to Break Through the Silence and Secrecy of Teenage Life *(cowritten with Gary Brozek), a handbook for parents looking to use Linderman's techniques to help them better communicate with their own troubled teens. In the following viewpoint, Linderman argues that* all *substance use by teens is abuse, because they are using substances as a dysfunctional—and ultimately destructive—way to satisfy fundamental psycho-emotional needs.*

As you read, consider the following questions:

1. According to the U.S. Surgeon General's Office, what are the four reasons teens drink, and what percentage drinks for each reason?

2. What chemical compound does the brain release as a result of drinking, and what are this compound's effects?

3. According to the National Survey on Drug Use and Health (NSDUH), how many Americans age twelve and older were current users of illicit drugs in 2005?

Among the . . . ways our kids act out as a result of emotional upheaval is the consumption of alcohol and drugs. It's hard for me to imagine, given all that we know about teens and drinking, that any parent could feel a sense of relief that their child is drinking and not doing drugs. I'm also stunned when parents are stunned to learn that their kids are experimenting with alcohol and drugs. And the number of kids who experiment with alcohol and drugs is not that far removed from the number of kids who abuse alcohol and drugs. I may be a bit of a hardliner when it comes to this issue, but I believe that any kid who is below the drinking age and who experiments with alcohol, who drinks sporadically or regularly, or who binges, is abusing alcohol. It's illegal for them to consume alcohol, so any teen consuming it in any way, shape, form, or amount is abusing it, in my estimation.

Teen Drinking Is a Widespread Problem

Legal and semantic issues aside, alcohol and drugs are a scourge preying on our kids. According to the 2004 (the most recent date for which this information was available) National Survey on Drug Use and Health (NSDUH) administered by the Substance Abuse and Mental Health Services Administration (SAMHSA), and the U.S. Department of Health and Human Services, alcohol abuse among young people follows a trend you'd likely imagine. Please note that I'm going to use the word "abuse" throughout, though the people at SAMHSA don't. They discovered that the prevalence of alcohol abuse increased as kids got older. Among adolescents age twelve, only 2.3% self-reported consuming alcohol (beer, wine, mixed drinks, straight liquor) in the thirty days before the survey. By age eighteen, that figure rose to slightly more than 50%. More disturbing are the percentages of young people who report that they engaged in binge drinking—five or more drinks on the same occasion—at least once in the previous thirty days. For twelve-year-olds, 1.1% of them responded "yes" to binge drinking—in other words, half of the twelve-year-olds who drink, binge. Slightly more than 41% of eighteen-year-olds admitted to binge drinking. The last category of consumption was heaving drinking—five or more drinks on the same occasion on at least five different days in the previous thirty days. Less than 1% of twelve-year-olds reported fitting in that category, but 15% of eighteen-year-olds did.

I don't want to belabor you with numbers, just show you the trend. I think it's noteworthy that for this survey at least, no significant statistical difference was noted by gender. Among young people age twelve to seventeen, 17.2% of males reported currently using alcohol, versus 18% of females. Interestingly, those who were attending college (eighteen-year-olds) or were employed were more likely to abuse alcohol than those who weren't attending or weren't employed. Also, alcohol abuse levels were higher in small towns and suburban areas than in major metropolitan areas. Many of the myths and stereotypes we may carry around as parents might be coloring our perceptions of who the "good" kids and "bad" kids are, where they live, and what their lives are like.

Teen Drinking Is a Dysfunctional Way to Satisfy Basic Needs

The U.S. Surgeon General's Office compiled a report on teens and drinking. Here are the conclusions drawn regarding why teens drink:

- 40% drink when they are upset.

- 31% drink when they are alone.

- 25% drink to get high.

- 25% drink when they are bored.

If teens' needs aren't being met, then they become confused, frustrated, angry, and in pain. To get rid of that pain, they take what our society tells them is an acceptable route to dulling that pain—they drink. Alcohol is the almost perfect solution, teens discover, to their problems. Of course, *we* know it's not a solution, but it does do a pretty good job of dealing with symptoms quickly. . . .

If there's one word I'd use to describe teens, it's "anxious." They tend to be impatient, and they tend to worry about their social standing, their grades, their appearance, their sexuality, and a host of other issues. If alcohol is good at one thing, it's good at reducing anxiety. . . .

Is it any wonder, then, that so many teens succumb to the temptation to drink? . . . Many of the teens I worked with, when asked why they drank for the first time and continued to drink, answered, "It was fun. There was nothing else to do. I had fun when I drank." Although it starts with that simple need, it grows more complex—and many teens don't understand all the needs that drinking meets. As parents we have to understand these needs and how they function in the lives of our kids.

Male Teens Feel They Need to Drink to Bond

For boys, and increasingly for girls, drinking is a rite of passage. How a young woman holds her liquor isn't a sign of her femininity, but how much a young man can drink certainly is a measuring stick used to determine masculinity. Now, I'm kind of an old fuddy-duddy in a lot of ways, and I don't want to believe this because I was some sort of all-American boy who believed my body was a temple and I didn't want to defile it with alcohol. After all, I was a jock, a football player. Well, today that attitude is anachronistic at best and laughable at worst. Among teens, male athletes drink more than nonathletes. We have a whole complex of associations among sports, alcohol, and men in this country, and many of our teenage and adolescent boys seek role models in athletes and their fathers. What do they see their fathers doing? Watching sports and drinking, perhaps? Teenage boys are firmly impressed by this mixed drink of alcohol, masculinity, and athletics, but I believe the connections extend beyond that.

Bill was a high school baseball player. While many of his friends first started to drink and experiment with drugs in middle school and junior high, Bill viewed himself the way I viewed myself at that age—as the all-American boy. He wouldn't be tempted. His father was a teacher at his school and also coached the basketball team. When Bill got to his senior year of high school, he decided he'd had enough of abstinence. He was tired of being left out of all the good times he was hearing about. Soon he became a fixture at all the parties. Bill would try to keep up with the boys, and he'd often drink to the point where he couldn't remember how much he had drunk. He began to ask a teammate to count for him. Bill was as competitive as could be, so he wanted to drink at least one more beer each night he went out drinking than he had on the previous occasion.

So, what's going on here that we can learn from Bill? First, drinking became a bonding experience. I've already said that it is a male rite of passage, and the camaraderie associated with drinking buddies and wingmen and all of that solidifies a young man's shaky standing among his peers. You may be a geek who doesn't know a zone press from hitting the cutoff man, but if you can drink, and drink a lot, you're okay in most jock's books—and let's face it, jocks tend to earn the highest status among teens.

Girls Want to Fit In, Too

Girls also frequently use drinking when their need for belonging goes unmet, but for girls, the results of this belonging often look quite different. As Rosalind Wiseman points out in her book *Queen Bees and Wannabes*, drinking allows girls to engage in activity, often sexual in nature, that they want to engage in (and sometimes don't), but they are too shy, awkward, and afraid to do so when not under the influence. Wiseman also points out that a girl can earn a positive reputation among her peers by consuming alcohol. Drinking someone under the table is not the sole province of males; the rewards (from a teen's point of view) are simply different. The world of teen drinking isn't fair to young women in this regard. A male who hooks up with a young woman while drinking, even if his peers view her as unattractive, undesirable, and beneath his standing, gets rewarded ultimately for his conquest. A young woman who engages in the same kind of behavior under the same set of circumstances and social standing gets punished with a bad reputation. Alcohol has the same numbing and erasing effects on teen women as it does on teen men, but somehow that eraser leaves a clearer afterimage behind when it's wielded by a woman. Not fair, but true.

Teen Boys Drink to Ease Emotional Pain and Isolation

For many teens who are suffering from the unmet need of freedom, consuming alcohol helps fill that void. Drinking can offer a freedom from expectations and the anxiety that surrounds those expectations. It can offer a temporary freedom, a freedom they think they need to express the true versions of themselves. With their inhibitions broken down, they can tell people how they really feel.

Not Even the Amish Are Immune

When Amish children turn 16, the rules change. They're encouraged to experiment and explore. The idea is that teens will come back to the church after tasting the modern world. For most this means a tentative foray—a trip to the local movie theater, or driving lessons. But for some, the experience, called rumspringa, is all about sex, parties and fast cars.

Tom Shachtman's new book *Rumspringa: To Be or Not To Be Amish* talks about how rumspringa works and what parents can learn from the Amish practice. . . .

> Around midnight, scores of Amish teenagers and twenty-somethings converge on the back acres of a farm. . . . Iced coolers of beer are put out; Amish teenagers reach for bottles with both hands. Young, mechanically adept men hook up portable CD players and boom-box speakers to car batteries. Shortly, rock and rap music blasts. . . .
>
> In one corner of the party, joints of marijuana are passed around, as are pipes of crank (crystal methamphetamine). Lines of cocaine are exchanged for money. A handful of the partygoers are seriously addicted, while others are trying drugs for the first time. Crank is incredibly and instantly addictive, and it is relatively simple and cheap to make; the only ingredient used that is not available from a local hardware store, anhydrous ammonia, is a gaseous fertilizer easily stolen from tanks on farms. Those few partygoers interested in doing hard drugs gather in a different location than the majority, who prefer drinking beer or smoking pot.
>
> *Tom Shachtman, "Rumspringa: Amish Teens Venture into Modern Vices," NPR, June 7, 2006, www.npr.org.*

This is especially true of young men who lack emotional fluency. Somehow, alcohol turns them—or at least so many young men believe it turns them—into articulate, expressive, sensitive souls. Any mothers reading this book will likely be able to recall at least one young man in her romantic history who expressed his undying devotion to her in an alcohol-fueled torrent. She can also probably recall a late-night, long-distance phone call from a would-be or once-was suitor who could thank his good buddy Jack Daniels [a popular brand of whiskey] for putting him up to it. For many teens, it is better to drink than to think. It is better to fuel than to feel. Alcohol, at least temporarily, numbs the pain of the social and emotional awkwardness that most teen boys feel—again, their lack of self-esteem comes into play.

In their best-selling book *Raising Cain: Protecting the Emotional Life of Boys*, Dan Kindlon, PhD, Michael Thompson, PhD, did an amazing job of lifting the veil of secrecy from an area of boys' lives that we seldom look at or talk about. As Kindlon and Thompson point out, alcohol is literally a pain reliever. It acts on the brain, and the body produces a compound very much like morphine. Our brains and bodies also do something similar when we exercise. You've probably heard of endorphins. Endorphins and the chemical response to drinking both produce opiates. Our opiate system is also involved with our emotions through our sense of touch. We feel comforted emotionally and physically when we are caressed, our skin is stroked, or we experience close bodily contact. All emotions are chemical in nature, so alcohol can serve as a substitute for the kinds of physical expressions of affection, compassion, and comfort that most kids, particularly males, no longer receive the way they once did as children and to a lesser degree as adolescents. If you are not comfortable with those kinds of physical displays of affection, and yet you crave them and need to fulfill your need for belonging, you can always find it in a bottle or a glass.

Teens Use Alcohol and Drugs to Excuse Mistakes

Not only does alcohol provide freedom from anxiety when someone is drunk, it also continues to offer that freedom the morning after. As the great eraser, alcohol offers a solution to the memory of awkward or embarrassing moments. One of the most painful things teens experience, and one of their greatest anxiety-producing fears, is being awkward and doing something stupid in front of peers or adults. Alcohol frees them from that fear. Christina . . . whose parents put extraordinary expectations for good behavior and success on her shoulders, once told me, "Mr. Mike, I had to do everything perfect to please my parents. One little mistake and they'd jump all over me. When I was with my boyfriend and we were drinking or smoking pot, I could say or do anything. If we were out with a bunch of his or my friends and we were drunk, we could do totally stupid things. Didn't matter. You could always say you were drunk. The perfect excuse for anything was, 'I was so wasted.'"

Teens can use that excuse to cover up a variety of sins, and whether they realize it or not, every time they use that justification, they feel as though it satisfies their need for freedom. They can have fun without any fear of embarrassment. When being wasted is their excuse, they can do whatever they want—or at least, that's what they think.

The Downside of Alcohol Consumption

With a few exceptions, it sounds as if I'm presenting you with a paid advertisement from the liquor and beer industry touting the beneficial effects of their latest cure-all. I'm no snake oil salesman, so I'll let you know the downside. As much as alcohol is that empowering, bond-creating, freedom-enabling substance, it is in fact a depressant. Ultimately, the fun high ends. For a lot of teens, especially those who binge drink, the depressive effects show up about the time they fall asleep, pass out, or, in the most severe cases, black out. (Studies show that three of ten high-school-age boys will pass out from too much alcohol at least once in their careers.)

As a result, they either are not aware of those depressive effects or figure they are a small price to pay for the benefits derived from alcohol. Unfortunately, sometimes those depressive effects are more serious. A recent [2007] incident in a suburb north and west of Chicago brought this painfully home to several young men and their families. According to a report in the *Chicago Tribune*, an eighteen-year-old boy was at the home of some friends, and toxicology reports later indicated that his blood alcohol content was over the legal limit, so the presumption was that he was drinking. Whether it was the depressive effects of the alcohol that made him say that none of their lives were worth living or not is difficult to say. Very likely it did contribute to his feelings and definitely contributed to what he did next.

Two of his friends tried to console him. Unfortunately, they didn't prevent him from getting behind the wheel of his car; instead they climbed in along with him. The disconsolate teenager then drove along a main highway, exceeding the speed limit considerably before veering off the road and crashing into the side of a building. One of the young man's friends was killed, while he and his other friend sustained serious injuries. Police investigators noted the absence of skid marks, interviewed those at the gathering who had heard the young man's remarks, and concluded that he intentionally drove off the road in the hope of killing himself. Instead, he killed a friend and now faces first-degree murder charges. . . .

Drinking to Be "Grown Up"

You may be saying to yourself that all of your teen's needs are met. He or she doesn't have to worry about survival, seems to have plenty of fun, enjoys freedom and power, and has a sense of belonging from plenty of friends. That may be true, but it doesn't mean that your teen won't drink. For many teens, consuming alcohol provides them with a privileged glimpse of the adult world. Year after year, they have probably heard you and teachers and others warning them about what these forbidden beverages can do. At the same time, they've likely witnessed adults drinking and seeming to enjoy themselves, and enjoying many of the benefits of alcohol I've previously discussed. Again, the temptation likely proves to be too much for them. They are at a stage in their lives when they want to become adults—not necessarily assume adult responsibilities, but enjoy the pleasures of being an adult.

To put it simply, even good kids do it. Even if you ensure that all of your kids' needs are met, they may still do it—the chances of them doing it are lesser but still there, but that doesn't mean that your cause as a parent is lost. [Although] many kids abuse alcohol, the difference between those who experience severe problems with the substance and those who don't is that those with problems are trying to fill one of their primary needs. Whether [that need] is fun, belonging, power, freedom—or, to a lesser extent, survival—problems with drinking can be the behavioral consequences of unmet needs in a variety of ways. . . .

Drugs Pose the Same Problems

Much of what was said above about alcohol and its ability to satisfy the unmet needs of your teen is true of drugs as well. I've used alcohol as an example throughout, but you can substitute the word "drugs" in most places, especially as it pertains to how the consumption of any type of drug serves the purpose of numbing pain, reducing inhibitions, providing an escape, and allowing your teen to feel a much-needed sense of belonging.

The good news, courtesy of the same NSDUH study I referenced for the numbers about alcohol consumption, is that illicit drug use is not on the rise among our young people. Here are the general conclusions and numbers provided by that study:

- In 2005, an estimated 19.7 million Americans age twelve or older were current (previous month) illicit drug users, meaning they had used an illicit drug during the month before the survey interview. This estimate represents 8.1% of the population age twelve years old or older.

- The overall rate of current illicit drug use among persons age twelve or older in 2005 (8.1%) was similar to the rate in 2004 (7.9%), 2003 (8.2%), and 2002 (8.3%).

- Marijuana was the most commonly used illicit drug (14.6 million previous month users). In 2005, it was used by 74.2% of current illicit drug users. Among current illicit drug users, 54.5% used only marijuana, 19.6% used marijuana and another illicit drug, and the remaining 25.8% used only an illicit drug other than marijuana in the previous month. Compare the 8.1% of teens abusing illicit drugs with the almost 50% abusing alcohol, and you can see why I put so much emphasis on drinking. Most parents agree that drug use is a serious issue. I'm not convinced all parents agree that consuming alcohol is a problem.

The trends we see among teen drug abusers are similar to those among teen drinkers. As teens grow older they are more likely to use drugs. In other words, more eighteen-year-olds use drugs than thirteen-year-olds do. Less than 4% of twelve- and thirteen-year-olds and slightly more than 22% of eighteen-year-olds reported using drugs. As you can see, your teen is far more likely to experiment with and use alcohol on a regular basis than they are [to experiment with and use] illicit drugs. Despite the alarm about the increasing use of methamphetamines (crystal meth), marijuana remains the drug of choice among abusers. That's not especially good news, since the potency of the marijuana available today is far greater than it was in previous decades. Males smoke marijuana only with a slightly greater frequency than females—a difference of just 1.2% overall across all ages.

All Drug Use Is High-Risk Behavior

For most teens, then, their consumption of illegal substances consists of alcohol and marijuana. Why teens choose to take other more powerful illicit drugs has less to do with which of their needs is being unmet than with the degree to which they feel the pain of that unmet need and a host of other factors. . . . For our purposes, the kinds of self-medicating our teens are doing is less important than the fact that they feel they have to self-medicate at all. Once we decide to treat all substance abuse as a high-risk behavior, very few if any differences exist. Getting to the reason . . . teens are abusing is more crucial than determining what they are abusing.

I'm not trying to diminish the seriousness of drug consumption. Instead, I'm trying to establish the importance of treating alcohol abuse with the same degree of tenacity and vigilance that we have illicit drugs. Though it was likely being implied in the "Just Say No" campaigns that talked about alcohol and illicit drugs, a bit of a wink and a nudge existed in our culture that told our kids that drinking was acceptable, because most of us have set that example for our kids. Perhaps it's time to refine that message. Also, it's time we let our kids know that while they may think of alcohol and drugs as the great need providers, they in fact create far more problems and needs than they solve.

> "A landmark study found that moderate experimentation with drugs character- ized the most psychologically healthy adolescents, while heavier use and ab- stinence were both signs of poorer ad- justment."

Little Teen Drug Use Is Abuse

Stanton Peele

Stanton Peele is a licensed psychologist and internationally rec- ognized expert on addiction who has written nine books on as- pects of substance addiction and compulsive behaviors. The fol- lowing viewpoint is drawn from his 2007 book Addiction Proof Your Child: A Realistic Approach to Preventing Drug, Alcohol, and Other Dependencies. *Writing primarily to parents who are concerned about their children's substance use, Peele argues that experimenting with drugs is normal, that little teenage substance use qualifies as addiction, and that even cases of abuse (which can be common, especially with alcohol and older teens) almost invariably recede on their own without intervention.*

As you read, consider the following questions:

1. Is gambling or sex addiction fundamentally different from drug addiction?

2. Is it helpful to tell teens with substance problems that addiction is a "disease" that he or she has inherited? Why?

3. What is the defining feature of an addiction?

The dominant—alarmist—view in America holds that children's substance use is horribly out of hand and aims for a future where no young people drink or take drugs. [Because] this state of nirvana has not yet been attained, then a fallback goal from this perspective is that youthful drug use be limited to high-risk children unlike your own—those who live on the wrong side of town.

The Problem of Alarmist Drug Education

American drug educators are virtually all of this alarmist school. It is impossible in the United States to acknowledge publicly that ordinary adolescents use drugs or drink and thrive anyhow. Nor is it possible for educators to discuss important research findings such as that moderate drinking reduces heart disease. The relentless message of school drug education, official proclamations about drugs, and statements by public figures is that all drug and alcohol use is bad and should be avoided by young people—that is, "just say no" or "zero tolerance." (Zero tolerance is the policy of suspending or expelling students who are found to use drugs or alcohol.)

The prevailing American view is that adolescents cannot manage—perhaps cannot even survive—using illicit substances. If young people actually use drugs and drink and turn out okay, this dirty secret should never be told. This position is patently absurd: [Our last three] presidents admitted using drugs or drinking heavily, and these admissions do not begin to plumb the depth of public figures' substance use. Nor do they capture your and your friends' drug and alcohol use when you were young. Adolescents, of course, recognize that such drug education is one-sided propaganda, and as a result, they usually turn off to all adult information on drug use and drinking.

At the opposite extreme from the alarmist point of view is what might be called the "benign" school. Since much of adolescent substance use is relatively harmless, since most children outgrow their problem use, since so many adults misuse alcohol and are now using illicit drugs and pharmaceuticals, some well-informed observers believe focusing on adolescent substance abuse is unwarranted.

My view incorporates elements of both of these positions but fundamentally disagrees with both. I believe the alarmist point of view is overstated. At the same time, I believe we need to encourage adolescents to recognize the actual risks of substance abuse and to reject regular intoxication in order to lead richer and fuller lives. Moreover, even though most young people don't develop a drug or alcohol problem, we must deal with reality and safeguard those who periodically misuse substances. This approach, called risk reduction, strives to prevent injuries or other damage that young people who become intoxicated either cause or suffer. . . .

The Problem Is Addiction, Not Drugs

People become addicted to experiences that protect them from life challenges they can't deal with. It is not possible to say that any one thing causes addiction. Most kids who use drugs and alcohol don't become addicted to them. On the other hand, they can get addicted to very typical, common activities—such as eating, the Internet, other media, games, even medications they are prescribed for other problems.

The core of an addiction is that people become enmeshed in an activity that interferes with their functioning and, for children, thwarts their growth. If your children avoid regular involvements and experiences, if they can't cope with their lives, and if you fear that, left to their own devices, they will either collapse or go haywire, your children face addictive problems.

Disagreements about the nature of addiction make for vast differences in how we go about combating it. I do not find it helpful to regard addiction as a disease, which is the prevalent view these days. Although many people, including scientists, now believe that a wide range of things can be addictive, they wrongly persist in seeing addiction as a biological phenomenon beyond people's control.

Drugs Are No More or Less Addictive than Sex or Gambling

By contrast, I was one of the first proponents of the view that addiction is not limited to drugs. But its very universality makes it clear that addiction can't be traced to a specific neurological mechanism. If sex or gambling addictions are defined by changes in the brain, why do so many people who find these involvements alluring for a moment, or even enthralling for some time, then simply move on to other activities? As we shall see, the exact same thing is true of "addictive" drugs.

Addiction can be especially debilitating for the young, but young people are more likely than not to outgrow it. The way out of addiction is to develop a range of skills and engage fully in life. The disease mythology is *particularly* unhelpful for young people. Telling adolescents that they have inherited addiction as part of their biological makeup encourages them to get stuck in the problem, rather than motivating them to overcome it.

Although my view of addiction is not the conventional one, my way of thinking has been adopted by many and is gaining influence in the field. My approach includes recognizing that addiction is not limited to drugs, that people overcome addiction when they are motivated and when their lives improve, and that successful therapy for addiction builds on people's own motivation to change while teaching them better ways of coping.

Expanding the Definition of Addiction

At the same time that not all drug use is addictive, addiction does not have to involve drugs. People can become addicted to powerful experiences such as sex, love, gambling, shopping, food—indeed, any experience that can absorb their feelings and consciousness. Addiction to the Internet is now in the spotlight, and before that came addiction to television and then video games.

Addictions provide quick, sure, easy-to-obtain gratifications, and advances in the electronic age such as the Internet, cell phone, iPod, and BlackBerry bring more addictive possibilities. Two addictions intertwined with the Internet are pornography and gambling. People become enmeshed in these experiences in isolation, rejecting everything else in their lives. A typical Internet pornography addiction case reads like this:

> My son is addicted to pornography. He can't stop looking at porn. He stays up on his computer all night. In the morning he can't stay awake and he often doesn't go to school. I'm at my wits' end.

Likewise, we frequently hear of people who cannot stop gambling or shopping, often going deeply in debt. Such addicts, as adults, may steal, go to prison, and lose their families as a result. . . .

Addictions Always Seriously Detract from Living Well

Watching television every night, drinking daily (for an adult), and having an active social life are not necessarily addictions. Broadening the definition of *addiction* does not mean that everybody is addicted to something. The word is now often used casually, even humorously: a friend says he is addicted to crossword puzzles, a baby is addicted to his pacifier, a teenager to her cell phone. . . .

People may joke that they are addicted to exercise or coffee or work, and they can be. But it is only when these things seriously detract from their ability to function that people are genuinely addicted—for example, they can't stop exercising after they have suffered an injury, or they drink coffee throughout the day even though it prevents them from sleeping, or they are so preoccupied with work that they neglect their families. . . .

For young people . . . the more connections to life they have, the better able they are to resist addiction. When people give up much of their lives for their addictions, it is because their other involvements are superficial or somehow unsatisfactory.

"Normal" Obsession to Addiction

We all rely on fixed elements in our lives, and children especially do. It is essential to your children's security and psychological well-being that you provide them with consistent limits, acceptance, and love. You should also recognize that children and adolescents will often fixate on an object or activity—their stuffed animal or a recording artist, playing with dolls or video games, wearing certain clothes or going to particular places. These fads are normal phases in growing up, and you should accept them as such.

What makes for addiction is when young people cannot extricate themselves from an activity in order to do the things required of them—things that they in some sense would *prefer* to be doing. Instead, they persist in behavior that is consistently harmful, or that is disapproved of by society, or that damages their health, their future, or their relationships with other people.

One of the thorniest problems for parents is deciding whether children are addicted when they use a substance (such as marijuana) regularly but otherwise function successfully. One possibility is that their drug use is normal. A landmark study found that moderate experimentation with drugs characterized the most psychologically healthy adolescents, while heavier use *and* abstinence were both signs of poorer adjustment.

> "Not so long ago, kids raided their parents' liquor cabinet when they wanted a quick high. Today, it's the medicine cabinet."

Teens Are Swapping Pills at "Pharming Parties"

Liz Doup

Liz Doup was among the first reporters to bring the new trend of "pharming parties" to national attention. At a "pharming party" teens gather to drink and indiscriminately swap and sample pharmaceuticals stolen—or "pharmed"—from their parents', grandparents', or friends' medicine cabinets. According to the 2009 Monitoring the Future survey—an annual survey conducted by researchers at the University of Michigan, which measures drug use attitudes and patterns among 50,000 eighth-, tenth-, and twelfth-graders—prescription and over-the-counter medicines account for more than half of all substances abused.

As you read, consider the following questions:

1. What was the percentage increase in adolescent prescription drug abuse between 1992 and 2005?

Liz Doup, "Teens Swapping Legal Drugs at 'Pharming' parties," *South Florida Sun-Sentinel*, May 5, 2006. Copyright © 2006, South Florida Sun Sentinal. Reproduced with permission from the Sun Sentinel.

2. Between 1992 and 2002, the U.S. population grew 13 percent; what was the percentage increase in prescriptions for controlled drugs during that period?

3. According to a Columbia University report, what percentage of prescription drug abusers also drink or take illegal drugs?

I n so many ways it sounds like any other teenage party.

Kids gathered in an abandoned Florida warehouse where strobe lights flashed and liquor flowed. But then from pockets and purses, the pills appeared.

Vicodin. OxyContin. Xanax. All legal drugs destined for illegal use.

2.3 Million Kids Are "Pharming"

Shannon Johnson, 17, a middle-school dropout, was part of the scene. He popped four or five Xanax, washed them down with vodka and was ready to party.

Not so long ago, kids raided their parents' liquor cabinet when they wanted a quick high.

Today, it's the medicine cabinet.

They're stocking up for "pharming parties," get-togethers sans [without] parents, where teens barter legal drugs and get high.

"It's better when you're with other people," says Shannon, a slender youth, lost in a pair of baggy jeans and oversized shirt. "I don't like doing this by myself."

There's nothing new about kids abusing prescription drugs. But pharming parties are a new social twist that contribute to the growing problem of prescription drug abuse, which has worked its way into pop culture via message boards, song lyrics and even T-shirts.

The number of users has mushroomed even as use of illegal drugs, such as heroin and marijuana, has decreased,

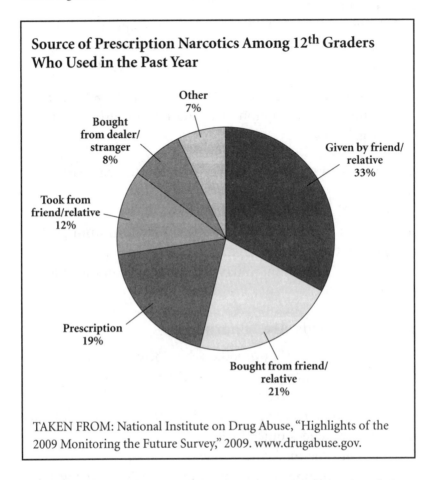

Source of Prescription Narcotics Among 12th Graders Who Used in the Past Year

- Other 7%
- Bought from dealer/stranger 8%
- Given by friend/relative 33%
- Took from friend/relative 12%
- Prescription 19%
- Bought from friend/relative 21%

TAKEN FROM: National Institute on Drug Abuse, "Highlights of the 2009 Monitoring the Future Survey," 2009. www.drugabuse.gov.

according to a report by Columbia University's National Center on Addiction and Substance Abuse.

The center says that about 2.3 million kids, 12 to 17, took prescription drugs illegally in the past year [2005], based on 2003 figures. That's a whopping 212 percent increase from 1992.

A False Sense of Safety

Shannon tumbled into the drug world at 10 with his first puff of marijuana. He's tried a cornucopia of drugs since, including Xanax from the family medicine cabinet, he says. But the kids who snag the family's pills share no cookie-cutter look.

"There's no specific group you can pinpoint," says Doris Carroll, community coordinator of the Palm Beach County (Fla.) Substance Abuse Coalition. "It's not just dropouts. It's not just popular kids. It's not just football players."

Much of the problem is linked to easy access, she says.

Indeed, some kids come by the drugs legally. Maybe they're taking Ritalin for attention deficit disorder or painkillers after losing their wisdom teeth or breaking a bone.

Others pillage [raid] medicine cabinets for forgotten pills. Some buy from kids. For others, drugs are a click away on the Internet.

"Kids think, 'It's not heroin. It's not crack. It's a legal drug. How bad can that be?'" says Barbara Zohlman, executive director of Miami-Dade's DFYIT (Drug Free Youth in Town), a school-based drug-prevention program.

In our quick-fix world, kids see adults, who'd never touch an illegal drug, fill prescriptions to treat everything from physical pain to anxiety. Meanwhile, pharmaceutical companies via TV and magazines hype drugs that promise a happier, thinner, more energetic you, all by popping a pill.

A Nation of Pill-Poppers

Between 1992 and 2002, while the U.S. population grew 13 percent, the number of prescriptions filled for controlled drugs—those with an abuse risk, such as morphine—increased by 154 percent, according to the study.

"We're a society of pill takers," Zohlman says. "We look at something to make us feel better rather than looking inside to make ourselves feel better."

Shannon slumps in a chair at the Starting Place, a treatment facility in Hollywood, Fla., where he's spending three months trying to shake his habit. Beside him sits Kyle Kahler, a fast-talking, energetic 16-year-old who squirms in his chair.

School dropouts at 14, they're both pharming party veterans. And addicts.

Kids like Shannon and Kyle can easily get addicted to painkillers, such as OxyContin, or anti-anxiety medicines such as Xanax. But even if their drug use doesn't land them in treatment, it can put them in the hospital.

When properly prescribed and taken as directed, opioids such as OxyContin safely relieve pain. Depressants, including Xanax, ease anxiety. And stimulants such as Ritalin increase attention and energy.

Dangerously Mixing Pharmaceuticals with Other Drugs

But taking such powerful drugs without supervision or mixing them with others, including alcohol, is a recipe for disaster. They can make breathing difficult or cause a rapid drop or increase in heart rate. They can impair senses so that everyday activities, such as driving a car, are hazardous.

In addition, kids up the danger factor by taking pills in unsafe ways. OxyContin, for instance, is supposed to be released into the bloodstream over several hours for long-term pain relief. But kids crush the pills for a quicker, and potentially more harmful, rush.

About 75 percent of prescription drug abusers also take other drugs or drink, according to the Columbia University report. Shannon and Kyle are no exception, routinely mixing legal pharmaceuticals with illegal drugs.

"You feel like you're on some kind of truth serum," says Kyle, who started smoking marijuana at 10 before moving on to prescription drugs as a teenager. "You have no inhibitions or fears. You feel like you can fight the biggest guy."

Getting the drugs is no problem. The boys buy from friends—OxyContin $12 to $15 pill or Xanax for $3. Valium goes for $4 to $5 a pop.

Sometimes kids trade with each other—a couple of Valium for a more powerful OxyContin.

At school or on the street, word of a pharming party drifts like smoke. Maybe they'll meet at someone's house when the parents are gone or rent a hotel room or find an abandoned warehouse.

Shannon was glad to be in the loop. When he got wind of a party, he wanted to be there.

"You're so much happier when you're f----- up," he says. "It's all good."

Compared with the rest of their peers, teens who abuse prescription drugs are:

- Twice as likely to use alcohol

- 5 times likelier to use marijuana

- 12 times likelier to use heroin

- 15 times likelier to use Ecstasy

- 21 times likelier to use cocaine

| "'Pharm party' is just a new label the drug-abuse industrial complex has adopted to describe the decades-old tradition of pill parties."

"Pharming Parties" Don't Exist

Jack Shafer

Jack Shafer is a writer, editor, and media critic for the liberal online magazine Slate. *Shafer often writes on media trends and national drug policy. He is especially noted for identifying and dismantling "bogus trend" stories. Since 2006, as an increasing number of "pharm party" reports surfaced in the media, Shafer has written a series of articles investigating the "pharm party" trend; he has never been able to confirm that any such parties exist—despite their prevalence in news reporting and television dramas—and sincerely doubts the widespread existence of parties where teens specifically gather to indiscriminately swap and pop pills.*

As you read, consider the following questions:

    1. According to a *USA Today* report, what is "trail mix"?

2. What research is Joseph A. Califano, Jr. citing when he talks about the "pharm party" trend in his introduction to the 2005 CASA report released by the National Center on Addiction and Substance Abuse at Columbia University?

3. What are four reasons that teens abuse prescription drugs, according to a 2005 CASA report?

Do "pharm parties" exist? . . .

In [a June 13, 2006 article] *USA Today* claims that drug-abuse counselors "across the USA" say they're "beginning to hear about similar pill-popping parties, which are part of a rapidly developing underground culture that surrounds the rising abuse of prescription drugs by teens and young adults."

Early Suspicions About the "New Trend"

[I] looked askance at the story, noting that the reporter hadn't witnessed a pharm party firsthand, nor had she interviewed a pharm party attendee, nor had she interviewed a police officer who had broken up one. Without a doubt, some teenagers do drugs. Without a doubt, some do drugs together. I'm certain that some of today's teenagers—like those from my generation (the 1960s)—even share drugs, including their own prescription pharmaceuticals or other licit drugs they've diverted from legal channels.

But pharm parties, where, "Bowls and baggies of random pills often . . . called 'trail mix,'" are dispensed, as *USA Today* reports? My BS detector started growling the minute I spotted the piece.

At the further prodding of a reader whose BS detector was also activated, I tracked the origin or the phrase "pharm party," aka "pharming parties." The earliest mention I found on Nexis and Factiva was from the March 8, 2002, Chambersburg, Pa., *Public Opinion*. The reporter writes:

With prescription drug abuse, the scene could be much different. In some communities, kids have "pharming" parties. They go to their parents' or grandparents' medicine cabinets and take whatever drugs are there. At the parties, they throw the pills in a bowl and take a handful, [Pamela] Bennett [a publicist for Purdue Parma, makers of OxyContin] said. The pills could be Viagra, antibiotics, blood pressure medication or anything else.

Again, the story quotes no teenage pharm partiers, interviews no witnesses to pharm parties, and cites no cop reports, etc. Next: A March 7, 2003, newsletter from the federal Center for Substance Abuse Prevention asserts that, "Students in big cities are 'pharming' these days—'pharming' being new lexicon for grabbing 'a handful' of prescription drugs and ingesting some of them or all of them." Note that the newsletter makes no mention of "parties," names no big city in which students actually engage in pharming, runs no interview with young pharmers.

A May 23, 2005, South Florida *Sun-Sentinel* op-ed, written by a local official from a substance abuse group, uses the phrase—"We hear stories about 'pharming' parties, where kids grab pills from a bag full of different prescription drugs, and [that] they have become popular at clubs, schools and homes." But she offers nothing beyond anecdotes.

Pharming doesn't break into the wider public conscience until the National Center on Addiction and Substance Abuse, or CASA, at Columbia University releases a July 7, 2005, press release. Written by its chairman, Joseph A. Califano Jr. ([President Jimmy] Carter's secretary of HHS [The U.S. Department of Health & Human Services]), it announces a 214-page report, *Under the Counter: The Diversion and Abuse of Controlled Prescription Drugs in the U.S.* Califano writes of "'pharming' parties where teens bring drugs from home and trade or share for purposes of getting high." Califano's sentence is repeated in the report's introduction.

There Is No Data Supporting the Trend

But is Califano citing CASA research about pharming parties? No, he's talking out of his hat.

"When Mr. Califano speaks of them in his quotes and statements, he is just referring to popular culture and today's trends," CASA spokesman Lauren R. Duran writes via e-mail. In a follow-up mail she writes:

> CASA does not have quantitative data on the subject of pharming parties, however we know that the trend exists based on focus groups we have conducted with teens and young adults for various CASA reports where we talk with them about prescription drugs at parties and this is the basis of Mr. Califano's quote.

Califano's comments about pharming parties received uncritical mention In the *Washington Post*, whose story was re-run by the *Toronto Star*, the *New York Sun*, and the State College, Pa., *Centre Daily Times*, among others. *Knight Ridder* newspapers, UPI, and the *Washington Times* also gave it non-skeptical treatment.

Time magazine cited the report in an Aug, 1, 2005, story. This one differs from the previous stories in that it describes actual drug trading among teens in a New Jersey basement—specifically, Ritalin for a painkiller. The reporter writes:

> This isn't an ordinary party—it's a pharming party, a get-together arranged while parents are out so the kids can barter for their favorite prescription drugs. Pharming parties—or just "pharming" (from pharmaceuticals)—represent a growing trend among teenage drug abusers.

A Name Coined by the Media

Note that the kids don't call it a pharming party, the writer does. And also note that *Time* claims that the parties "represent a growing trend among teenage drug abusers." Evidence of the trend, reports *Time*, comes in the fact that "about 2.3

million kids ages 12 to 17 took legal medications illegally in 2003, the latest year for which figures are available."

The source of *Time's* data? The CASA report. But if you consult page 46 of CASA's report where the data are presented, you learn something significant about the 2.3 million teens who admitted to having taken legal drugs illegally. "Not all teens and young adults who abuse prescription drugs do so to get high," CASA states, "Some abuse these drugs to relieve stress, relax or to improve their academic performance." Does that sound like a party—pharm or otherwise—to you?

The story gets its next major press bump from the *Sun-Sentinel* in a widely reprinted April 23, 2006, article. Reporter Liz Doup cites the 2.3 million figure from CASA. She also watches teenagers swap pharmaceuticals—Vicodin, OxyContin, Xanax—at a warehouse party where liquor flows. In an e-mail interview, she acknowledges that none of the drug-using teenagers she interviewed used the phrase "pharm party" or "pharming parties."

"Those using the term 'pharming parties' were people involved in drug education and treatment," Doup explains.

Teens Don't Seem to Play Any Part

On the entertainment front, two network TV dramas exploited pharm party plot lines—*CSI-NY* in November 2005 and *Boston Legal* in May 2006—perhaps increasing the phrase's profile.

Even so, MySpace—the online mecca for teenage networking and socializing—is pretty quiet about pharming parties. MySpace contributors are known for 1) their youth and 2) for their willingness to post almost anything. A targeted search of MySpace using Ice Rocket reveals just 16 mentions of "pharm party," and none for "pharming party." A Technorati search grabs 15 mentions of "pharm party" and just seven mentions of "pharming party." If pharm parties are a trend, they're the best-hidden and least-talked about one in the country.

It goes without saying that pharm parties may be very real and very everywhere. It's a big country. But it looks to me like pharm party is just a new label the drug-abuse industrial complex has adopted to describe the decades-old tradition of pill parties.

For those who thought *USA Today* milked the pharm dry, CASA delivered a new bale of cow-fattening hay today (June 19, 2006): a new white paper titled *"You've Got Drugs!" Prescription Drug Pushers on the Internet: 2006 Update.* It comes with a press release by Califano in which he states with more certainty than evidence that:

> The trend of teen "pharming parties" will continue to increase as long as these drugs are so easy to obtain.

Addendum, June 20, 2006: I failed to reach the author of *Time*'s pharming party story, Carolyn Banta, before deadline. In an interview today she says that "two or three" of the 15 or so attendees at the party described in her story spontaneously referred to the event as a "pharming party," without any prompting from her. "My assumption is that they probably heard it from a popular culture reference," Banta says. Banta also says that her interest in the subject was sparked by the CASA report of July 2005.

> *"Even when they see it's having harmful effects on their lives, with their relationships, with their schoolwork, with their ability to perform athletics—they may not be able to stop."*

Marijuana Is Very Bad for Teens

Karen Fanning

Karen Fanning is a frequent contributor to Scholastic Choices *magazine, which is dedicated to covering "issues involving family life, consumer awareness, careers, personal responsibility, substance abuse prevention, nutrition, and more" in a way that fosters complex analysis and critical thinking among students. In the following viewpoint, the author describes the lasting physical, personal, social, and legal repercussions of adolescent marijuana use. According to the 2009 Monitoring the Future survey, teen marijuana use has gradually increased over the past several years, while teen disapproval of marijuana use and perception of the risks of marijuana have steadily declined.*

Karen Fanning, "Marijuana Mess: Six Years Ago, This Teen Smoked Marijuana for the First Time. Before Long, He Was Hooked on the Drug and Breaking the Law to Support His Habit," *Scholastic Choices*, vol. 24, issue 6, April–May 2009, pp. 9–14. Copyright © 2009 Scholastic Inc. Reproduced by permission of Scholastic Inc.

As you read, consider the following questions:

1. How many young people try marijuana for the first time each day?

2. Marijuana is naturally occurring; according to the article, does that mean that it is safe?

3. How many chemicals does marijuana contain?

Michael Wilson [name changed to protect his privacy] was 12 years old the first time he smoked a marijuana joint. "All of my friends were smoking," Michael, now 18, tells *Choices*. "The way people were talking about it, they glamorized it. It was something I wanted to try. I wanted my friends to accept me."

That experience began a terrible time in Michael's life. Within a month, he was smoking marijuana every day, often getting high as soon as he got out of bed in the morning. His abuse of marijuana led him to start dealing drugs, which resulted in his eventual arrest. In short, drug abuse almost ruined Michael's life.

A Drug Abused Daily by Thousands

Marijuana is the most widely used drug among teenagers in the United States. Every day, nearly 3,600 young people smoke marijuana for the first time. While most will not become addicted to marijuana, the National Institute on Drug Abuse (NIDA) estimates that one in 10 people will become dependent on the drug.

"Even when they see it's having harmful effects on their lives with their relationships, with their schoolwork, with their ability to perform athletics—they may not be able to stop," says Susan Weiss, chief of the Science Policy Branch at NIDA.

Michael, who is from Paterson, New Jersey, mistakenly believed that marijuana wasn't harmful. "Because it grew on land, I thought it was OK," he says, in other words, Michael thought that because marijuana comes from a plant, it was a natural product that was safe.

Marijuana and Tobacco Pose Similar Health Risks

Weiss counters that "tobacco is from a plant too, and it's obviously not healthy." Marijuana smoke contains many of the same chemicals as tobacco. But because it is inhaled more deeply, it takes just one joint to expose your lungs to the same amount of cancer-causing chemicals and carbon monoxide found in four or five cigarettes.

Medical research hasn't confirmed that smoking marijuana increases the risk of getting lung cancer, but there is no doubt that marijuana use contributes to chronic coughing, more chest colds, and a higher risk of getting a lung infection.

Marijuana contains nearly 400 chemicals. The main ingredient is delta 9-tetrahydrocannabinol, or THC. Today's marijuana contains about 8 percent THC—compared with 2 to 3 percent in the mid-1980s—making the drug more potent than ever.

THC binds to the cannabinoid receptors in the brain. These receptors are found in areas of the brain that influence movement, coordination, perception, memory, thinking, and concentration. Marijuana can disrupt all of these functions.

Marijuana Inhibits Cognitive Abilities

Once in your body, marijuana slows down reaction time and interferes with coordination. As a result, your ability to play sports suffers. Even worse, your ability to drive a car is adversely affected. The National Highway Traffic Safety Administration reports that even a small amount of marijuana impairs your ability to drive.

Marijuana inhibits your ability to think, concentrate, and problem solve too. It's no wonder that marijuana use is linked

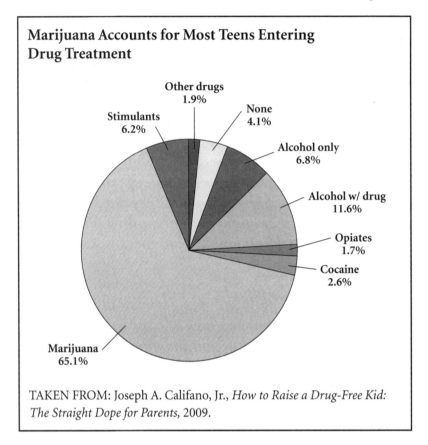

Marijuana Accounts for Most Teens Entering Drug Treatment

Other drugs
1.9%

None
4.1%

Stimulants
6.2%

Alcohol only
6.8%

Alcohol w/ drug
11.6%

Opiates
1.7%

Cocaine
2.6%

Marijuana
65.1%

TAKEN FROM: Joseph A. Califano, Jr., *How to Raise a Drug-Free Kid: The Straight Dope for Parents,* 2009.

to poor academic performance. Once a good student, Michael lost interest in school. He was lucky to make it to class twice a week, and his grades dropped to D's and F's.

"I just lost focus of everything," Michael says. "School was boring. I used to like going to church. Smoking marijuana drew me away. I was a DJ and I stopped DJing. I couldn't even focus on that. I just wanted to get my next high, to find more money to smoke."

A Habit That Creates Criminals

To support his habit, Michael stole money from his mother and then began selling drugs. In the fall of 2007, Michael was selling crack cocaine, and unbeknownst to him, the police were watching.

"The cops were watching me with binoculars," he says. "They caught me in the act of selling."

Michael was arrested and eventually sent to the New Jersey Training School for Boys, a prison for youth offenders that was nearly two hours from his home. He was able to see his mother and siblings only every other week. "I was so far away from home," Michael says. "I was shocked to be there. I was just lost."

During the 10 months he was locked up, Michael had no choice but to get clean. At the end of his sentence, prison officials asked Michael if he wanted to enter a drug rehabilitation program. He said yes because he didn't want to relapse once he returned home.

Challenges to Sobriety

"I wanted to be out there living my life and not using drugs," Michael says. "I wanted to function without being high. I wanted to enjoy myself without being high."

Michael is currently living at Integrity House, an adolescent substance-abuse treatment facility in Newark, New Jersey. He is working toward finishing high school and getting his driver's permit.

He has three months to go in his stay at Integrity House but a lifetime ahead as a recovering drug addict. "Everyone knows I used drugs," Michael says. "I will have to change who I hang out with, where I go, and what I do. I will have to make new friends. I'm going to do that. My life will revolve around positive people."

*"Pot-smoking teens tend to function at
better levels than teens who also smoke
tobacco, and better in some ways than
kids who abstain from both."*

Marijuana Is Not Dangerous
to Most Teens

Tim King

*Tim King has more than twenty years of news reporting experi-
ence and is the founder of Salem-news.com, where this viewpoint originally appeared in 2007. In the following viewpoint,
the author cites the findings of a 2007 Swiss study published in
the* Archives of Pediatric & Adolescent Medicine, *which found
that adolescents who used marijuana were more socially driven
and significantly more athletic than either their peers who
smoked tobacco or peers who abstained from both tobacco and
marijuana. The marijuana-smoking teens also performed about
as well academically as their peers, even though they were more
likely to skip classes.*

As you read, consider the following questions:

1. According to this Swiss study, what drawbacks are associated with smoking marijuana?

2. Both the Swiss study and a similar study done in New Zealand, found an increased level of cannabis use was associated with what?

3. According to the article, can a cross-sectional study, like this Swiss study, be used to ascertain cause and effect?

They cut class and don't always have the best relationships with their parents, but youth today who smoke cannabis may not face the perils suggested by traditional institutions.

The oldest continuously published pediatric journal in the country, a journal of the American Medical Association called the *Archives of Pediatrics & Adolescent Medicine*, has released new information indicating that pot-smoking teens tend to function at better levels than teens who also smoke tobacco, and better in some ways than kids who abstain from both.

Study Overturns Old Stereotypes

Completed in Switzerland, the study also found that those who use only cannabis were more socially driven and showed no more psychosocial problems than those who had never taken either of the substances.

As far as marijuana leading to harder drugs, the authors of the study say [in] an accurate listing . . . the problems actually fall in a different order, and that cancer-related illnesses suffered by cigarette smokers are the biggest risk of all.

"The gateway theory hypothesizes that the use of legal drugs (tobacco and alcohol) is the previous step to cannabis consumption. However, recent research also indicates that cannabis use may precede or be simultaneous to tobacco use and that, in fact, its use may reinforce cigarette smoking or lead to nicotine addiction independently of smoking status."

The study, conducted by J.C. Suris, M.D., Ph.D., University of Lausanne, Switzerland, and team, examined information from a 2002 national survey involving 5,263 Swiss citizens aged 16–20 years. Four-hundred-fifty-five smoked just mari-

Exaggerating Risks Costs Credibility

"If I tell my 15-year-old that he's going to have a psychotic episode if he smokes pot, but he knows that his older brother already smokes pot and is fine, is he going to believe me when I tell him that methamphetamine damages the brain?" asks Mitch Earleywine, an associate professor of psychology at the State University of New York at Albany. . . . Amphetamine psychosis is an established effect of taking large doses of that class of drugs; warnings about it appear on the labeling of prescription amphetamines. "What's going to happen," says Earleywine, "is we're going to lose all credibility with our teens."

Maia Szalavitz, "The Return of Reefer Madness: The U.S. Drug Czar's Office Is Running Ads Implying That Smoking Marijuana Can Lead to Insanity. But Pushing Dubious Science Is No Way to Persuade Teenagers Not to Do Drugs," Salon.com, September 19, 2005.

juana, while 1,703 smoked both tobacco and marijuana. Another 3,105 students in the study had never used either substance.

A Study with Several Surprising Findings

Some Go Without a Cigarette—Characteristics of Cannabis Users Who Have Never Smoked Tobacco, finds that, "Interestingly, our results do not confirm our hypothesis of better overall functioning among abstainers. In fact, what our research indicates is that the main difference between COG (cannabis-only group) youth and abstainers is that the former are more socially driven: they are significantly more likely to practice sports, and they have a better relationship with their peers."

The article says there are some drawbacks, and one of those is an effect on school attendance. But overall, the study indicates few notable problems in the youth who smoke marijuana.

"Even though they are more likely to skip class, they have the same level of good grades; and although they have a worse relationship with their parents, they are not more likely to be depressed. Nevertheless, our results seem to indicate that, although typical of the adolescence process, having good support from friends together with a less solid relationship with parents is a risk factor for occasional cannabis use."

The study says abstainers, kids who have never used cannabis or other illegal drugs, "were less socially engaged and had a stronger orientation toward school."

It confirms that substance use, at least tobacco, alcohol, and cannabis, is largely used by adolescents for socializing purposes. [The researchers] suggest that this fact could explain the difference between COG youth and abstainers regarding peer relationships.

Correlating Substance Use and Social Acumen

Other findings indicate that having a good relationship with a best friend was related to increased use of cannabis, alcohol, and tobacco.

Similarly, it was reported that although abstainers are successful in many social arenas, "they socialize less frequently with friends than youth who drink," while a Finnish study indicated that, "moderate use of alcohol among adolescents was associated with a positive self-image in social relationships."

This information would undoubtedly apply differently in the United States, where trends have moved toward zero tolerance in recent years, with no legal options for legal underage drinking. Many European nations are more tolerant on this issue.

Another study referenced in the article . . . was performed in New Zealand. [It] also indicated an association between a high level of connectedness to friends and an increased level of smoking and use of cannabis in the previous month.

"In addition, and contrary to previous research," the study states, "our study does not confirm the negative effect of cannabis on academic performance among COG youth. In our case, they are more likely to be high school students and they report similar grades as abstainers, even though they skip class more often."

Cannabis Use Still Linked to Increased Drug Use

However, they say that compared with abstainers, COG adolescents are more likely to have been drunk or to have used illegal drugs in the previous month.

"Although this finding might be part of the exploratory behavior this specific group seems to have, there is research indicating that compared with nonusers, cannabis users nave more frequent access to other drugs, such as [3, 4]-methylene-dioxymethamphetamine (Ecstasy)."

But on the other hand, the findings indicate that these youth who use cannabis tend to have a worse relationship with their parents than abstainers.

"Because their school results are not worse, it could be hypothesized that the worse relationship they have with their parents is more likely due to their drug consumption."

Limitations to the Study

They say the main strength of their study is that it is based on a nationally representative sample of adolescents.

"Nevertheless, some limitations need to be stressed. First, the cross-sectional nature of our survey does not allow us to ascertain causality [in other words, this study cannot prove that marijuana use causes, or is caused by, these other behaviors]. Second, although technically youth in the nonsmoking group do not smoke cigarettes, we do not know from our data whether they use tobacco to prepare their cannabis cigarettes. Third, school dropouts, who are known to be heavier substance users, were not included in the study. Fourth, because our data are self-reported, there is always room for speculation about the honesty of the answers. However, the fact that the questionnaire was anonymous should minimize any reporting bias."

The study cautions that while the results confirm that CTG (cannabis and tobacco group) youth tend to present psychosocial problems at a higher rate than COG youth and as such constitute a potential target for preventive interventions, the fact that COG youth, compared with abstainers, seem to do at least as well, if not better, in some areas raises 2 questions.

"First, those adolescents who only use cannabis but who may also use some tobacco to prepare their cannabis cigarettes should be advised about the possibility of becoming addicted to nicotine. Second, because the step between being an occasional or a regular cannabis user is not well established, this specific group of adolescents should also be counseled and closely monitored over time. In any case, and even though they do not seem to have great personal, family, or academic problems, the situation of those adolescents who use cannabis but who declare not using tobacco should not be trivialized."

The *Archives of Pediatrics and Adolescent Medicine*, formerly known as the *American Journal of Diseases of Children*, is the oldest continuously published pediatric journal in the country, dating back to 1911. It is an international peer-reviewed journal published 12 times per year as a Journal of the American Medical Association.

> *"Young people and experts who monitor drug use agree that meth is steadily replacing marijuana as the teenage drug of choice."*

Teen Meth Use Is Increasing

Martha Irvine

Martha Irvine has reported for the Associated Press for more than a decade. Her writing focuses on issues important to teens and young adults, ranging from fashion trends to vital social issues. In the following viewpoint, Irvine highlights the impact the methamphetamine epidemic has had on the U.S. Midwest, and especially on teens. Because methamphetamine can be cheaply produced from relatively common ingredients under rudimentary conditions, its use has spread widely in rural and economically depressed areas, where it has become increasingly attractive to teens, both for its powerful effects and low price.

As you read, consider the following questions:

1. What percentage of girls in Minnesota alternative schools used methamphetamine in 2004?

2. Name three visible physical results of meth use.

3. How many states have passed laws to control the sale of cold medicine that can be used to make methamphetamine?

They sit at a cafeteria table, gossiping and snacking during a school field trip. "Have you seen him? Has he gained the weight back?" one girl asks. "Yeah, he looked so good," replies another from across the table. "His cheeks filled in." It's no casual lunchtime conversation. The teen they're talking about is a recovering methamphetamine addict—and so are several of the teens at the table, all of them students who attend alternative high schools in the St. Paul area and who are trying to get their lives back on track.

While the methamphetamine epidemic has often been associated with drug labs hidden away in the countryside, today's users frequently defy that image, whether they are urban professionals or suburban homemakers.

Minnesota has been dealing with all of the above and is home to another scary trend: Here, many young people and experts who monitor drug use agree that meth is steadily replacing marijuana as the teenage drug of choice.

"Meth is THE thing—it's what everybody wants to do," says Anthony, a 17-year-old Student at Sobriety High School in St. Paul, who first tried meth at age 13 and has been in recovery since he overdosed last summer. He and other students from alternative learning programs were allowed to speak on the condition that their last names not be used.

While statistics show that meth use among teens and middle-school students has been level for the past few years, experts caution that those numbers can be deceiving, since meth seems to spread in pockets, leaving some regions or populations relatively untouched while others are devastated.

"Meth is an oddball in that way," says Caleb Banta-Green, an epidemiologist at the University of Washington's Alcohol & Drug Abuse Institute. "You never know where it's going to hit."

But when it does, it often hits hard—with few states evading meth's reach in one population or another, including young people.

In Nebraska, for instance, two 20-year-olds who were high on meth froze to death after getting lost in a snowstorm in January. And in Oregon, officials recently reported that meth is now second only to marijuana—surpassing alcohol—as the drug that sends the most teens to treatment in that state.

Nebraska and Oregon are among the nearly two dozen states that have entrenched meth problems, most of them in the West and Midwest, according to state-by-state advisories the Drug Enforcement Administration released this year. And the DEA says meth is a growing concern in sections of nearly every other state.

"It's here and it's ravaging our kids," says Dave Ettesvold, a drug counselor at two high schools in the St. Paul area, including Harmony Alternative Learning Center in Maplewood.

Already in Minnesota, a fifth of addicts who entered drug treatment for meth use last year were younger than 18, according to Carol Falkowski, a researcher at the nonprofit Hazelden Foundation, who tracks the state's drug trends for the National Institute on Drug Abuse.

Another recent state survey found that about a quarter of girls and a fifth of boys in Minnesota's alternative learning schools had used meth at least once in the last year. Ten percent had used it 10 times or more.

How teens get methamphetamine varies. Sometimes, they say friends or relatives—even a parent—get them into it. Some have sold meth to pay for their own habit. And a few say they eventually learned how to make the drug themselves.

Kristin, a 17-year-old student at Harmony, tried meth a little more than a year ago while smoking pot in a friend's basement, as the friend's parents slept upstairs.

"Have you ever tried 'crystal'?" he asked, bringing out crystal methamphetamine and a small glass pipe that some refer to as a "bubble."

She hadn't tried it, but told her friends otherwise: "I said, 'Yeah' and just went along with it."

She says the reasons teens are attracted to meth are many, from a wish to lose weight, especially for girls, to the euphoric feeling users get when they first take the drug—a feeling that ends up causing them more trouble than it's worth, she adds.

Many other teens say they also like the long-lasting effects, including an "in control" feeling and the ability to focus and stay up for hours.

"I just felt invincible," says Summers, a 15-year-old student at Harmony, who got her first hit of meth at age 13 from a friend's drug-dealing older brother. "You feel like you're better or stronger than everybody."

Like Kristin, she smoked the drug, which also can be injected, snorted or taken orally. But she quickly became so hooked that "if it fell on the chair, I'd lick it off the chair."

It didn't take long for the effects—emotional and physical—to turn ugly.

"I'd look in the mirror and my face would look yellow. I'd say, 'I gotta stop for a while or my mom will find out,'" Summers says, recalling how her mom cried when she finally figured out what was going on. Her mother had asked if she was doing meth but, until she was in rehab, Summers never admitted it.

Indeed, the physical effects of methamphetamine use are often jarring—from sunken eyes and bone-thin frames to teeth that turn gray and deteriorate.

One juvenile court counselor still carries teeth that a young meth user gave to her to show other teens who might be considering taking the drug. "Her teeth literally fell out on my desk when she was talking to me one day," says Beverly Roche, who was working with the juvenile drug court in Minnesota's

Meth Brutalizes the Children of Rural Oelwein, Iowa

Oelwein [Iowa] chief of police Jeremy Logan, reflecting a reality nationwide, readily admits that law enforcement dismantles, at most, one in ten of the total number of [meth] labs in existence. Extrapolate that onto the number of children taken out of Iowa meth labs alone in 2003 and 2004 (700) and that means that at least 7,000 kids were living every day in homes that produce five pounds of toxic waste, which is often just thrown in the kitchen trash, for each pound of usable methamphetamine. . . .

[Nathan Lein, assistant prosecutor for Fayette County, Iowa] estimated that 95 percent of all his cases were related to the drug in one manner or another: manufacture and distribution, possession, possession with intent to distribute, illegal sale of narcotics to a minor, driving under the influence of an illegal substance, etc. Of those, he had to offer a plea in about ninety-eight out of a hundred, he said. What bothered him most were the crimes, and these were numerous, in which children had been involved. Many of those included child rape. Others involved neglect to an order of magnitude—three-year-olds left alone for a week to take care of their younger sibling; children drinking their own urine to avoid dehydration—that had once been unheard of in Oelwein.

Nick Reding, Methland:
The Death and Life of an American Small Town, *2009.*

Dodge County, southeast of the Twin Cities, at the time. She's now helping establish a juvenile drug court with programs aimed at rehabilitating young people who use meth and other drugs in Chisago County, north of St. Paul.

Changes in behavior also are very common, with many meth users becoming edgy, aggressive and paranoid.

Anthony, the 17-year-old from Sobriety High, spent so much time high on meth and sitting by his bedroom window—afraid the police or someone else was out to get him—that friends started calling him "Garfield," a reference to the stuffed toy version of the cartoon cat that people stick on windows with suction cups.

Bettylu, an 18-year-old student at Harmony, was scared into quitting the drug after watching her older, meth-using sister become violent. She says the sister also had trouble caring for her young child.

"If you keep using it, there will be no responsibility left," Bettylu says.

Karen LaBore, a mother from nearby Forest Lake, knows what she means.

LaBore was one of dozens of people who gathered in recent weeks for a community meeting about meth in Chisago County, where officials are considering opening their own "sober" high school in response to the growing drug problem there. The meeting—one of many that grass-roots community groups are organizing across the country—brought residents together with law enforcement officials, social workers, school counselors and drug experts from the Hazelden Foundation, which is based there.

Her voice shaking, LaBore had a warning for other parents. She told the group about her 27-year-old daughter, who she says has been using meth for years. LaBore is now raising her daughter's three young children and worries about the effect meth might have on them and her own 12-year-old son.

"We need to learn how to protect our kids," she said. "We have to get to these kids before they start this."

To that end, she has started a local chapter of the group Mothers Against Methamphetamine, or MAMa, which meets each week at her church.

Meanwhile, many Minnesotans are pinning their hopes on a proposed law that would make it difficult for anyone to buy large quantities of cold medicine that contains pseudoephedrine, a main ingredient in meth. A few states, including Oklahoma and Illinois, have already passed such laws.

Spencer, a 15-year-old from St. Paul who is currently in rehab for meth and cocaine use, thinks the proposal would be a good start. But as one who's relapsed and returned to drug use several times in his short life, he knows how tough it can be to battle meth.

"It's going to be hard to get rid of it," he says, shaking his head. "Really hard."

> "Since the advent of measurement of methamphetamine use by high-school seniors, lifetime, yearly, and daily trends have shown an aggregate decline."

There Is No Meth Epidemic

Ryan S. King

Ryan S. King is a policy analyst for the Sentencing Project, a nonprofit advocacy organization "working for a fair and effective criminal justice system by promoting reforms in sentencing law and practice, and alternatives to incarceration." The following viewpoint is drawn from a report analyzing the reality of the "meth epidemic" purportedly destroying our communities, straining law enforcement and welfare systems, and specifically targeting the young. According to the author, methamphetamine use is actually declining—even among teens—and continues to represent a minuscule percentage of drug arrests and hospital admittances. King also contends it is as responsive to evidence-based treatment as any other addictive substance.

Ryan S. King, *The Next Big Thing? Methamphetamine in the United States*, Washington, DC: The Sentencing Project, 2006. Copyright © 2006 by The Sentencing Project. Reproduced by permission.

As you read, consider the following questions:

1. According to the 2004 *National Survey on Drug Use and Health*, what portion of all Americans over the age of twelve were regularly using methamphetamine?

2. What is the difference between a "lifetime" meth user and a "regular (monthly)" meth user? Why does the author argue that, even as the "lifetime" meth user number continues to climb, there is no meth epidemic?

3. According to the University of Michigan *Monitoring the Future* survey, how much has the lifetime prevalence of high school seniors reporting meth use dropped?

Methamphetamine is a dangerous drug that represents a substantial challenge to policymakers, health care professionals, social service providers, and the law enforcement community. Over time, methamphetamine abuse can result in the deterioration of physical and mental capacities, the dissolving of family ties, diminished employment prospects, and a lifetime spent cycling through the criminal justice system. The consequences of irresponsible drug abuse harm not only the individual, but his or her family and the larger community. Thus, it is important that our public resources be effectively directed to both *prevent* the development of such a habit as well as *treat* those individuals before the proverbial die has been cast.

Scare Tactics Undermine Prevention

Unfortunately, the American strategy of drug control since the early 20th Century has emphasized an approach of *prevention* based on instilling fear about a substance through dramatized descriptions and images of the consequences of use coupled with a notion of *treating* people with harsh punishments out of step with the harm caused by the drug. Historically, the domestic response to drug use has been to demonize the drug and the people who use it while exaggerating the impact of its use ("You'll be hooked the first time you try it"). This strategy has been complemented in the past two decades with mandatory minimums, sentencing enhancements, and a ban on access to services such as public housing, income assistance, and federal educational aid as the result of a drug conviction.

Historian David Musto suggests that the incongruity between what people were told about drugs and personal experiences had a critical impact on public perceptions about drug policy beginning in the 1960s. As more people tried drugs and realized that many of the horrific consequences did not result, a mistrust of government statements about drug use began to emerge. There is evidence suggesting that this approach of "prevention through scare tactics" not only fails to diminish drug use, but may undermine public education efforts. . . .

The findings of this report refute the image of methamphetamine use in the United States as popularly conveyed by both the media as well as many government officials. Mischaracterizing the impact of methamphetamine by exaggerating its prevalence and consequences while downplaying its receptivity to treatment succeeds neither as a tool of prevention nor a vehicle of education. To the contrary, this combination of rhetoric and misinformation about the state of methamphetamine abuse is costly and threatening to the national drug abuse response because it results in a misallocation of resources. We urge vigilance in tempering our national response to methamphetamine, keeping the focus local and providing federal funding to augment evidence-based treatment protocols that have been demonstrated successful in a number of jurisdictions.

Nationally, Meth Use Is Infrequent

Both national use rates as well as criminal justice data belie the emergence of a methamphetamine epidemic. Regular and lifetime use figures, rather than suggesting widespread addiction, demonstrate that the vast majority of people who use methamphetamine do so infrequently. Only a fraction goes on to become regular users, and for those individuals there are a number of promising treatment options. . . .

Nationally, use of methamphetamine, as collected by the *National Survey on Drug Use and Health (NSDUH)*, has been steady over the past five years [since 2001]. Methamphetamine remains a drug used by a very small proportion of Americans. In 2004, 0.2% (583,000) of Americans over the age of 12 were regular users of methamphetamine. The frequency of methamphetamine use is similar to [that of] crack cocaine, near the lowest levels of regular drug abuse. The percentage of monthly methamphetamine users, the best proxy for individuals who are likely to have a substance abuse problem, is 1/4 that of cocaine users and 1/30 of marijuana users. Meanwhile, the number who report binge drinking in the last month is more than 90 times the number who report methamphetamine use in the last month.

Lifetime use rates, which are frequently used when ascribing descriptors such as "epidemic" and "plague" to methamphetamine use, provide an imprecise reflection of how many people are *currently* [in 2006] using the drug. In 1999, 9.4 million Americans reported having used methamphetamine in their lifetime, a doubling of the number from a 1994 study. By 2004, the lifetime number had increased to nearly 12 million. By any account, this rapid growth in lifetime users could, and has, raised alarms among the public. However, between 1999 and 2004, the proportion of all methamphetamine users who were regular (monthly) users increased only slightly, from 4.6% to 5%. The distinction is that even one-time users are still considered lifetime users, although they clearly do not suffer from current substance abuse.

Historic trends in methamphetamine use do not suggest the development of a looming problem. In 2004, 1.44 million Americans over the age of 12 had used methamphetamine in the past year, and 583,000 were regular users. The Substance

Abuse and Mental Health Services Administration (SAMHSA) only recently began to collect regular, systematized figures on methamphetamine use in 1999, but . . . it is apparent in those six years of data collection that monthly use rates have remained steady. . . .

Meth Use by High Schoolers Is in Decline

Concern has been expressed that the impact of methamphetamine abuse may be particularly acute for young people, who are considered most vulnerable to the negative consequences of drug abuse. The University of Michigan's *Monitoring the Future* (MTF) study surveys 8th-, 10th-, and 12th-graders about tobacco, alcohol and illicit drug abuse. As with the NSDUH study, MTF did not begin to administer systematic measurement of methamphetamine use until 1999. Trends over the last six years [c. 2000–2005] of data collection indicate that, as with the total adult and juvenile population annual and monthly methamphetamine use among high school students has also been steady since 1999.

Usage patterns of high-school seniors are good indicators of cautionary developments that might affect adult drug abuse patterns. Since 1999, the lifetime prevalence of high school seniors reporting methamphetamine use dropped by 45% from 8.2% to 4.5% in 2005. During that same period, the annual prevalence figures declined from 4.7% to 2.5%, while daily figures remained steady between .1% and .2%. Thus, since the advent of measurement of methamphetamine use by high-school seniors, lifetime, yearly, and daily trends have shown an aggregate decline.

The authors of the report note the incongruity between the results of the analysis and the common perception of use patterns, and suggest that perhaps the school-based survey instrument is missing individuals who have dropped out from school and may have higher rates of use. If that were the case, the national survey data of persons 18 to 25 years of age

Methamphetamine Abuse Facts

- Methamphetamine is among the least commonly used drugs
- Only 0.2% of Americans are regular users of methamphetamine.
- Four times as many Americans use cocaine on a regular basis and 30 times as many use marijuana.
- Rates of methamphetamine use have remained stable since 1999
- The proportion of Americans who use methamphetamine on a monthly basis has hovered in the range of 0.2–0.3% between 1999 and 2004.
- Rates of methamphetamine use by high school students have declined since 1999
- The proportion of high school students who had ever used methamphetamine (lifetime prevalence rates) declined by 45% between 1999 and 2005, from 8.2% to 4.5%. . . .
- Drug treatment has been demonstrated to be effective in combating methamphetamine addiction
- Studies in 15 states have demonstrated significant effects of treatment in the areas of abstention, reduced arrests, employment, and other measures.
- Methamphetamine abuse has generally been shown to be as receptive to treatment as other addictive drugs.
- Misleading media reports of a methamphetamine "epidemic" have hindered the development of a rational policy response to the problem
- Media accounts are often anecdotal, unsupported by facts, and at odds with existing data.
- Exaggerated accounts of the prevalence, addictiveness, and consequences of methamphetamine abuse risk not only misinforming the public, but may result in a "boomerang effect" in which use and perception are negatively affected.

The Sentencing Project,
The Next Big Thing? Methamphetamine
In the United States, *www.sentencing.project.org, June 2006.*

would be a good place to observe any spikes in use. . . . Data from the NSDUH show generally steady monthly use rates for 18- to 25-year-olds during the period of 1999–2004. The slightly higher rates than the general population are to be expected because this is a younger age cohort [group]; however, the trend is virtually identical to general use rates. . . .

The Role of the Media in the "Meth Epidemic" Myth

Media coverage of methamphetamine—both of its prevalence and the consequences of its abuse—has increased substantially in the last five years. The common thread that runs through this coverage is that methamphetamine is unique in terms of addictiveness and consequences of use relative to other drugs. An official from the Office of National Drug Control Policy referred to methamphetamine as "the most destructive, dangerous, terrible drug that's come along in a long time." The governor of Montana described the situation in his state with the following warning: "It's destroying families; it's destroying our schools; it's destroying our budgets for corrections, social services, health care . . . [w]e're losing a generation of productive people. My God, at the rate we're going, we're going to have more people in jail than out of jail in 20 years."

The media has picked up on this theme, routinely referring to a methamphetamine "epidemic." Recent coverage of methamphetamine in the press has followed a generally formulaic approach that may include: leading with anecdotal stories that distort national trends in methamphetamine use, mischaracterizing the consequences of use and receptivity to treatment, and warnings of an impending invasion of methamphetamine in jurisdictions in which current use is rare. These stories are framed in such a way as to support a preconceived notion or theory about methamphetamine, and as such, dissenting viewpoints and critical assessment are seldom pursued. Common to many stories are the inclusion of predictions of dire consequences, often in the person of officials speaking about issues for which they lack expertise. For example, a law enforcement officer stating that methamphetamine addiction is impossible to treat. A general lack of critical analysis coupled with widespread reporting of opinions masquerading as facts have resulted in a national media that has been complicit in perpetuating a "myth of a methamphetamine epidemic."

Reporting Graphic Anecdotes Instead of Solid Facts

Many news outlets have portrayed methamphetamine as America's most threatening "boogeyman," frequently making sweeping statements as to the drug's prevalence, addictive properties, and consequences while failing to provide documentation or foundation for these claims beyond a quote or two. Emblematic of this brand of coverage is the following: "Methamphetamines have become the drug of choice across the nation and the 'one hit and you're hooked' drug is one of the hardest for health officials to treat and users to kick." That opening line of an article from a New Mexico newspaper has the distinction of offering three separate statements unsupported by fact (methamphetamine as the drug of choice, it only takes one "hit" to become addicted, and it is more difficult to treat than other drugs).

Many media outlets have been guilty of grossly distorting methamphetamine use trends, often using a single case to illustrate an emerging "pattern" posited in the article. In August of 2005, *Newsweek* featured a cover story calling methamphetamine "America's Most Dangerous Drug," in which it described methamphetamine use as an "epidemic" and a "plague," while observing that it has "quietly marched across the country and up the socioeconomic ladder." Beginning with a story about an upper-middle class family, the article describes the downward spiral of a woman who lost everything due to her methamphetamine addiction and eventually was arrested for operating a meth lab. The obvious implication of this story is that if this can happen to a "good" family with two children, a six-figure income, a dog and a Volvo in the garage, then it can happen to anyone.

However, absent anecdotal stories and a handful of sensationalist quotes, the article fails to substantiate the claim posited in the title. This scenario, of methamphetamine use "march[ing] across the country," is not corroborated by any evidence. No statistics are provided to support the theme of a methamphetamine epidemic, no data indicates that methamphetamine is more dangerous than any other drug, and no regional statistics illustrate this purported cross-national "march" of methamphetamine. In place of data, the article liberally employs quotations intended to convey the gravity of the situation. The ominous conclusion suggests grim prospects for the future, noting "like the addiction itself, this epidemic can only be arrested, not cured." The source for this assertion is neither a law enforcement expert nor a treatment professional; rather, it is the opinion of a 46-year old former methamphetamine dealer. . . .

Teens and Meth in the Media

In some cases, media stories about methamphetamine present contradictions within the same article. For example, a South Carolina newspaper ran a story about youthful methamphetamine users, stating that "[e]xperts say meth . . . is starting to show up in the littlest addicts." The theme of the article was that the risks of methamphetamine are now threatening the most vulnerable population: adolescents and pre-adolescents. The article predictably begins with the story of a 13-year-old who tried methamphetamine at the age of 12 and is now in a rehabilitation center and recovering from a suicide attempt. The article continues by suggesting that the region is experiencing a "disturbing [methamphetamine] trend," evidenced by the recent arrest of five area teens for possession of methamphetamine with intent to distribute. Further investigation into this arrest indicates that two of the teens were 18 and the other three were 17. This is not to downplay the offense, but rather to highlight that this collection of "teens" are at a very different level of maturity than the featured 13-year-old.

Regarding the "emerging problem" of youthful methamphetamine use, the story does note that national data indicate that methamphetamine use is leveling off. Actually, although not mentioned in the story, recent data suggest it is declining in the population featured in this article. That fact notwithstanding, two treatment experts are cited as suggesting, absent any supporting evidence, that there is a significant threat lurking regarding juvenile methamphetamine use. The article states that "counselors are afraid that *eventually* [emphasis added] even more teens will experiment with meth," while a representative of Child Protective Services admits that her office has not removed any children from domestic situations in which methamphetamine was present, "but she knows that the drug is out there." No rationale is given to support their fear of increasing teen use rates. These remarks, and the story as a whole, illustrate a general paranoia regarding methamphetamine that results in people ascribing validity to unsubstantiated fears while ignoring empirical data. This irrationality both fuels and is fueled by the media, which responds to sensationalist claims about trends and consequences by printing alarming stories of "epidemics" and "crises," while in turn perpetuating a widespread misperception that these claims are fact. In a self-fulfilling feedback loop, this increases public susceptibility to believe the epidemic mythology.

Periodical Bibliography

The following articles have been selected to supplement the diverse views presented in this chapter.

Elizabeth Bernstein "Teens Favor Painkillers, Alcohol and Marijuana over Stimulants," *Wall Street Journal Health Blog*, December 11, 2008. http://blogs.wsj.com.

John DiConsiglio "'Little Girl, You Are in Big Trouble': Samantha Martin Never Thought Her Substance-Abuse Problem Would Catch Up with Her—Until She Was Arrested on Drug Charges," *Scholastic Choices*, January 2009.

Ryan S. King, Joe Dunn, Maia Szalavitz, and H. Westley Clark "How Bad Is the U.S. Meth Problem?" NPR.org, June 14, 2006.

ScienceBlog "Study Says Marijuana No Gateway Drug," December 4, 2006. www.scienceblog.com.

Jack Shafer "The Worst 'Pharm Party' Story Ever," Slate.com, March 17, 2010.

Maia Szalavitz "The Return of Reefer Madness," Salon.com, September 19, 2005.

Sharon Worcester "Survey: Teens Use Inhalants More, Worry About Risks Less," *Clinical Psychiatry News*, June 2006.

OPPOSING
VIEWPOINTS®
SERIES

CHAPTER 2

Does Alcohol Pose a
Special Threat to Teens?

Chapter Preface

In contrast with other drugs, alcohol can be legally produced, sold, and consumed by most Americans, and is
deeply ingrained in many Americans' lifestyles, religious ob-
servances, and cultural traditions. So, it comes as little sur-
prise that alcohol abuse, especially among teens and young
adults, seems to be an especially persistent and widespread
problem in the United States.

For example, parents and university officials alike bemoan
the fact that, as reflected in a 2009 report published in the
*Journal of the American Academy of Child and Adolescent Psy-
chiatry*, there has been little change in binge-drinking behavior among college-age males since 1979. Even more troubling,
binge drinking has actually increased notably among young
women both in and outside a campus setting. Confusingly,
other studies indicate that alcohol consumption has actually
steadily *decreased* among 18 to 25 year-olds since 1980—a
trend that matches the established decline in alcohol-related
auto accidents in that age bracket, as well as the general downward trend in drug use of all kinds by young adults. Furthermore, most research shows that those binge-drinkers—while a
concern—are a small fraction of college students: 81 percent
of full-time undergrads drink moderately or abstain completely.

Some researchers—most notably David J. Hanson, a professor emeritus of sociology at the State University of New
York at Potsdam who has studied alcohol and drinking behavior and policy for more than 40 years—point out that the
term "binge drinking" itself had badly confused the issue.
Prior to the 1990s, the term "binge drinker" was commonly
used to describe a person who drank debilitatingly, behaved
recklessly and neglected normal responsibilities for a period of
days or even weeks. In the early 1990s Harvard University

School of Public Health professor Henry Wechsler launched his College Alcohol Study, bringing the epidemic of "college binge drinking" to light. But for the purposes of his study, Wechsler refined the definition of "binge drinking" to "the consumption of five or more drinks in a row for men and four or more for women at least once in the past two weeks." This clear departure from the established notion of a "drinking binge" did not take into account the drinker's ultimate level of intoxication, the apparent impact on judgment and behavior, or even the duration over which the drinks were consumed. So, although there may be exactly as many "binge drinkers" today as there were in 1979, it is almost certain that those drinkers are consuming far less alcohol, and wreaking much less havoc.

The authors of the following viewpoints explore the unique impact alcohol has on American culture and health, and they discuss how to best address alcohol abuse among teens.

| *"The legal drinking age seems to be less important than the culture and practices surrounding alcohol."*

It Is Healthy for Teens to Drink Moderately in the Home

John Buell

John Buell is a regular columnist with the Bangor Daily News *who has written often on the issue of underage drinking. In this viewpoint, the author argues that it is hypocritical to have the legal drinking age set three years higher than the age of majority (i.e., eighteen, the age at which most U.S. teens qualify to drive, serve in the military, marry, and engage in legally binding contracts of all types). He notes that teen binge drinking is the result of a broader dysfunctional attitude toward alcohol that can best be addressed by teens learning to drink moderately with their families.*

As you read, consider the following questions:

1. According to the author, why are there no bingeing epidemics in Middle Eastern theocracies?

John Buell, "Thoughts on Underage Drinking," *Bangor Daily News*, June 13, 2006. Reproduced by permission of the author.

2. According to Brown University anthropologist Dwight Heath, what drinking etiquette do Southern European parents teach their teens?

3. The author states that binge drinking often arises among the children of what group of American parents?

My critics are certain that teens are uniquely damaged even by modest amounts of alcohol. Yet if readers accept this argument, they must still acknowledge that alcohol is only one of many risks teens face. Is the sedentary 18-year-old who (legally) smokes a pack of cigarettes a day at less risk of serious disease than the 18-year-old athlete who drinks a beer at dinner every night? How do the risks of soda or high-fat diets compare?

The Hypocrisy of a Drinking Age Above the Age of Majority

Many citizens suspect that culture and power rather than science drive decisions to criminalize certain groups and substances. Nor have my critics convinced me that jail terms for parents and storekeepers will be more effective than such draconian steps were in the 1920s.

The new prohibition fails to acknowledge the ambivalent place of older teens in our culture and is inattentive to the context in which teen and adult pathologies emerge.

Parents who are convinced that any alcohol injures teens should share this view with them. But ratcheting up a legal attack on "underage drinking" is problematic. In our society, parents properly rear children in the expectation that by 18 or even younger they will be independent adults able to weigh risks and rewards.

The United States is guilty of two glaring hypocrisies regarding teens. Political leaders claim concern for teen health, yet they allow and sometimes encourage teens to take risks when it suits adult society. Teens are free to die in Iraq or be-

Teen Binge Drinking on a Steady Decline

While a continuing barrage of newspaper articles, TV shows, and special interest group reports claim that binge drinking among young people is a growing epidemic, the actual fact is quite to the contrary. Binge drinking among young people is clearly declining and it has been doing so for many years. . . .

"Binge" drinking among high school seniors has declined from 41.2% to 27.9% between 1980 and 2003.

David J. Hanson,
"Binge Drinking," Alcohol Problems & Solutions,
www2.potsdam.edu/hansondj.

come low-wage managers working at convenience stores in the wee hours of the night. Just as fundamentally, adults routinely take varying degrees of risk for their own pleasure. No reader of this paper [The *Bangor Daily News*] fears automobiles more than I, yet I commute to Ellsworth [Maine] to play tennis. I could reduce my risk of a car crash and could achieve comparable aerobic benefits working on my stationary exercise bike at home.

Nonetheless, in today's legal climate, a 19-year-old veteran who has a beer at his 18-year-old fiancée's home exposes himself to fines and her parents to jail time. Such double standards invite contempt. Ironically, they also send the message that alcohol is the most coveted symbol of adulthood.

Worldwide, Attitudes Toward Teen Drinking Vary

There are societies where teen drinking is almost nonexistent.

In Middle Eastern theocracies [governments under religious rule], adults do not drink. Consequently, there is no teenage drinking epidemic.

Police states that abhor independent minds of all age and have contempt for pleasure in most forms will eradicate underage drinking.

Critics counter that a lower drinking age in some European social democracies has produced an epidemic of alcohol abuse. World Health Organization data, however, indicate huge differences among European states with similar drinking ages.

The legal drinking age seems to be less important than the culture and practices surrounding alcohol.

Even one prominently featured article in the recent [2006] *New York Times* critique of underage drinking, from the *Archives of Pediatric and Adolescent Medicine*, comments: "Italy, France, Portugal and Greece had similar or smaller percentages [of teen binge drinkers] than the United States. Whether young people in those countries are more likely to drink with family and in meal settings and whether such practices moderate risks posed by early drinking warrant study."

Developing a Culture of Moderation

Such study is under way. Brown University anthropologist Dwight Heath has identified characteristics of several Southern European subcultures where teens legally drink as early as 16 but binging and the violence that often accompanies excess are much less common. These cultures teach their teens something many American politicians can't grasp—the difference between moderation and abuse. Teenagers have two equally acceptable options: (a) to abstain or (b) to drink in moderation. Parents do more than remove car keys. They teach and model in their lives the lesson that abuse of alcohol at any age is totally unacceptable.

In the U.S. context, a recent study in the *Journal of Adolescent Health* by Dr. Kristie Long Foley provides survey data showing that drinking alcohol with parents reduces teen binge drinking. It teaches teenagers responsible drinking habits and extinguishes some of the novelty of drinking.

Moralistic Obsession Trumps Social Welfare

I have one caveat. The more thoughtful U.S. studies present a distressing pattern. Alcohol abuse often emerges among risk-prone children with stressed, overworked and impoverished parents. Adding to their burdens, these children often attend inadequate schools. Some binge, receive no help and become addicted at an early age. The cultures with fewer drinking problems are less workaholic and offer more support for families. Unfortunately, however, Western European welfare states and the religious movements that have reduced economic inequality, limited working hours and enabled family life are breaking down.

Some of these welfare states have been stridently nationalistic and have also imposed narrow understandings of the family. It remains to be seen whether more inclusive and cross-national citizen alliances to curb corporate exploitation, give adults some security, and [whether they] support vulnerable children that can be fostered. Unfortunately in the United States, moralistic obsessions and attacks on vulnerable minorities stand in the way of such agendas, as in the '20s.

| "No matter what the reason, parents who are overly permissive, or who encourage teen drinking, put their children at risk."

The Dangers of Allowing Children to Drink at Home

Joseph A. Califano Jr.

Joseph A. Califano Jr. is the founder of CASA, the Center on Addiction and Substance Abuse (now called the National Center on Substance Abuse). From 1977 to 1979, Califano served as the U.S. secretary of Health, Education, and Welfare. The following viewpoint is drawn from his 2009 parenting guide How to Raise a Drug-Free Kid: The Straight Dope for Parents. *Califano stresses that, despite popular opinion in some circles, there is no scientific research that indicates that "acclimating" a teen to alcohol via supervised drinking in the home prevents teen binge drinking, prevents alcohol abuse or reckless drinking.*

As you read, consider the following questions:

1. What is the only European country with a lower rate of teen binge drinking than the United States?

Joseph A. Califano Jr., *How to Raise a Drug-Free Kid: The Straight Dope for Parents*, New York, NY: Fireside Books, 2009, pp. 61–65. Copyright © 2009 by Joseph A. Califano Jr. Reproduced by permission of Fireside Book, an imprint of Simon & Schuster Macmillan.

2. What are "social host" laws?

3. What does research from the Center for Addiction and Substance Abuse indicate is the best course of action to prevent teen drinking?

The public health messages is: It is not okay for children to drink alcohol at all until they are adults, and then only in moderation. While all states prohibit selling or furnishing alcohol to anyone under twenty-one, most states make an exception that allows parents to provide alcohol to their children in their homes or (in some states) in a public place.

Supervised Drinking Does Not Prevent Teen Bingeing

But as a parent, you may be conflicted about what rules you should set about your teens' drinking with the family. You may wonder if all teen drinking is bad. What about small amounts at family celebrations, or at Christmas dinner? Will allowing them to drink small amounts with you teach your children to drink moderately as adults?

I will provide you with some parenting examples to consider, but how you set limits on alcohol depends very much on your knowledge of the effect of alcohol on your teen and your assessment of what will work best for your child.

Some parents believe that the best way to teach their children to use alcohol responsibly as adults is to start teaching them to drink responsibly when they are young. Parents may begin giving their children watered-down wine or small sips of beer in the tween or early teen years, gradually increasing the portion to half a glass of wine at special dinners or at family celebrations when their children are in their late teens. Parents who embrace this approach generally believe that their children will learn to drink responsibly as adults if they practice limited drinking at home as teens.

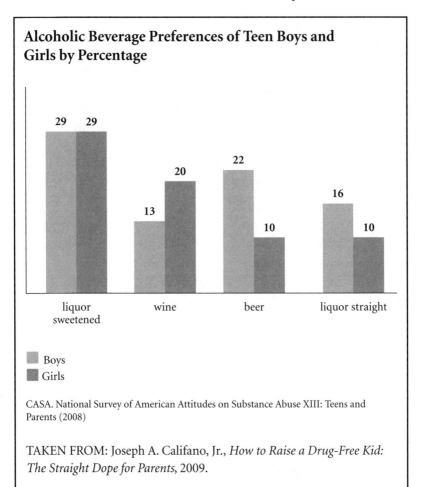

Alcoholic Beverage Preferences of Teen Boys and Girls by Percentage

CASA. National Survey of American Attitudes on Substance Abuse XIII: Teens and Parents (2008)

TAKEN FROM: Joseph A. Califano, Jr., *How to Raise a Drug-Free Kid: The Straight Dope for Parents*, 2009.

There is no scientific research to support the idea that allowing your children to drink at home will prevent them from binge drinking outside the home. In Europe, many countries have no minimum drinking age; in those that do, the minimum age is usually between sixteen and eighteen. Studies have shown that in virtually every European country except Turkey (which is Muslim) teens binge drink at higher rates than in the United States. The rate of binge drinking among teens in Ireland, Germany, the UK, and Switzerland is more than twice the rate of binge drinking among teens in the U.S. The rate in Denmark is even higher.

Supervised Drinking Does Not Reduce Alcohol's Allure

Some parents believe that it is better to have the kids drinking under their roof than to have them drinking and driving. Other parents may be unable or unwilling to assert authority over their teens. No matter what the reason, parents who are overly permissive, or who encourage teen drinking, put their children at risk. Teens who believe that their parents will not care if they are caught drinking are more likely to drink, binge drink, and use other substances.

Another belief that underlies permissive parenting practices is that forbidding alcohol entirely will only encourage teens to drink more and to drink clandestinely. There is no evidence that letting your children drink at home will discourage them from drinking elsewhere. Nor is there any evidence that telling your teenager that he is not allowed to drink will encourage him to do the opposite.

Allowing other parents' children to drink alcohol in your home is likely to violate one or more "social host" laws. These laws, which many local jurisdictions are enacting, hold persons who are over twenty-one criminally responsible for such underage drinking that occurs in their home.

Fear of Punishment Reduces Teen Drinking

As a parent, you can learn all the facts about alcohol, but parenting is really about doing what's best for your kid. Your child is a precious individual, not a statistic. It is your job to decide what rules will work for you and your family. In making the decision regarding what message to give your children on alcohol, consider your long-term objectives. When it comes to drinking, it is more important that your children don't damage their brains, become addicted, or accidentally kill themselves by drinking too much than that they think of you as a cool parent. For every year that you're able to postpone your child's first use of alcohol, your child's risk of becoming dependent on alcohol goes down.

While I can't tell you what rules will work best for your teen, I recommend that you set dear limits that teens should not use alcohol, or at least not unless they are drinking on some special occasion with you, stick to those limits when your teen pushes against them, and enforce them with consequences when your teen violates them.

Realistically, it may be difficult to prevent your teen from ever drinking alcohol. Your teen is prone to risk-taking. This is normal teenage behavior. Even if you expect that your child will drink underage, don't make it easy for him to do so. CASA [Center for Addiction and Substance Abuse] research shows that teens who are closely monitored and supervised, who believe that their parents will catch and punish them if they are caught drinking, are less likely to drink. In fact, teens want their parents to establish and enforce limits. Despite any protest otherwise, remember: Your teen really does want you to be a parent.

If you decide to allow your child to try alcohol under your supervision, a little wine at Christmas or a family celebration, you should take steps to ensure that your child is not drinking outside your home without your supervision.

| "The principal problem of 2009 is not drunken driving. The principal problem of 2009 is clandestine binge drinking."

The Drinking Age Should Be Lowered

John M. McCardell Jr.

John M. McCardell Jr. is president emeritus of Middlebury College and the founder and president of Choose Responsibility, a nonprofit organization fostering open public debate of the repercussions—intended and unintended—of having the drinking age set at twenty-one. Here McCardell notes that the drinking age was raised to twenty-one as a response to startlingly high rates of teen drunk driving in the 1970s (at that time each state set its own drinking age, typically age eighteen or nineteen). As of 2009, the United States is the only industrialized nation in the world with a drinking age as high as twenty-one.

As you read, consider the following questions:

1. According to a 2009 study published in the *Journal of the American Academy of Child and Adolescent Psychia-*

try, how have binge drinking rates for college-age males, women attending college, and women not attending college changed since 1979?

2. How many underage drinkers die every year because of alcohol?

3. What other nations have a drinking age of twenty-one? What are the most common drinking ages?

One year ago [in 2008], a group of college and university presidents and chancellors, eventually totaling 135, issued a statement that garnered national attention.

Underage Drinking Is on the Rise, Despite the Law

The "Amethyst Initiative" put a debate proposition before the public—"Resolved: That [age 21 as the minimum] drinking age is not working." It offered, in much the way a grand jury performs its duties, sufficient evidence for putting the proposition to the test. It invited informed and dispassionate public debate and committed the signatory institutions to encouraging that debate. And it called on elected officials not to continue assuming that, after 25 years, the status quo could not be challenged, even improved.

One year later, the drinking age debate continues, and new research reinforces the presidential impulse. Just this summer [2009] a study published in the *Journal of the American Academy of Child and Adolescent Psychiatry* revealed that, among college-age males, binge drinking is unchanged from its levels of 1979; that among non-college women it has increased by 20 percent; and that among college women it has increased by 40 percent.

Remarkably, the counterintuitive conclusion drawn by the investigators, and accepted uncritically by the media, including editorials in the *New York Times* and the *Washington Post*, is that the study proves that raising the drinking age to 21 has been a success.

More recently, a study of binge drinking published in the *Journal of the American Medical Association* announced that "despite efforts at prevention, the prevalence of binge drinking among college students is continuing to rise, and so are the harms associated with it."

Worse still, a related study has shown that habits formed at 18 die hard: "For each year studied, a greater percentage of 21- to 24-year-olds [those who were of course once 18, 19 and 20] engaged in binge drinking and driving under the influence of alcohol."

Changing a Culture of Drunk Driving

Yet, in the face of mounting evidence that those young adults age 18 to 20 toward whom the drinking age law has been directed are routinely—indeed in life- and health-threatening ways—violating it, there remains a belief in the land that a minimum drinking age of 21 has been a "success." And elected officials are periodically reminded of a provision in the 1984 law that continues to stifle any serious public debate in our country's state legislative chambers: Any state that sets its drinking age lower than 21 forfeits 10 percent of its annual federal highway appropriation.

But it's not 1984 anymore.

This statement may seem obvious, but not necessarily. In 1984 Congress passed and the president signed the National Minimum Drinking Age Act. The act, which raised the drinking age to 21 under threat of highway fund withholding, sought to address the problem of drunken-driving fatalities. And indeed, that problem was serious.

States that lowered their ages during the 1970s and did nothing else to prepare young adults to make responsible decisions about alcohol witnessed an alarming increase in alcohol-related traffic fatalities. It was as though the driving age were lowered but no drivers education were provided. The results were predictable.

Addressing a New Problem

Now, 25 years later [in 2009], we are in a much different, and better, place. Thanks to the effective public advocacy of organizations [such as] Mothers Against Drunk Driving, we are far more aware of the risks of drinking and driving. Automobiles are much safer.

Seatbelts and airbags are mandatory. The "designated driver" is now a part of our vocabulary. And more and more states are mandating ignition interlocks for first-time DUI offenders, perhaps the most effective way to get drunken drivers off the road.

And the statistics are encouraging. Alcohol-related fatalities have declined over the last 25 years. Better still, they have declined in all age groups, though the greatest number of deaths occurs at age 21, followed by 22 and 23. We are well on the way to solving a problem that vexed us 25 years ago.

The problem today is different. The problem today is reckless, goal-oriented alcohol consumption that all too often takes place in clandestine locations, where enforcement has proven frustratingly difficult. Alcohol consumption among young adults is not taking place in public places or public view or in the presence of other adults who might help model responsible behavior. But we know it is taking place.

Clandestine Binge Drinking

If not in public, then where? The college presidents who signed the Amethyst Initiative know *where*. It happens in "pre-gaming" sessions in locked dorm rooms where students take multiple shots of hard alcohol in rapid succession, before going to a social event where alcohol is not served. It happens in off-campus apartments beyond college boundaries and thus beyond the presidents' authority; and it happens in remote fields to which young adults must drive.

And the Amethyst presidents know the deadly result: Of the 5,000 *lives lost to alcohol* each year by those under 21, more than 60 percent are lost OFF the roadways, according to the National Institute of Alcoholism and Alcohol Abuse.

The principal problem of 2009 is not drunken driving. The principal problem of 2009 is clandestine binge drinking.

That is why the Amethyst presidents believe a public debate is so urgent. The law does not say drink responsibly or drink in moderation. It says don't drink. To those affected by it, those who in the eyes of the law are, in every other respect, legal adults, it is Prohibition. And it is incomprehensible.

A Drinking License

The principal impediment to public debate is the 10 percent highway penalty. That penalty should be waived for those states that choose to try something different, which may turn out to be something better. But merely adjusting the age—up or down—is not really the way to make a change.

We should prepare young adults to make responsible decisions about alcohol in the same way we prepare them to operate a motor vehicle: by first educating and then licensing, and permitting them to exercise the full privileges of adulthood so long as they demonstrate their ability to observe the law.

Licensing would work like drivers education—it would involve a permit, perhaps graduated, allowing the holder the privilege of purchasing, possessing and consuming alcohol, as each state determined, so long as the holder had passed an alcohol education course and observed the alcohol laws of the issuing state.

Most of the rest or the world has come out in a different place on the drinking age. The United States is one of only four countries—the others are Indonesia, Mongolia and Palau—with an age as high as 21. All others either have no minimum age or have a lower age, generally 18, with some at 16.

Young adults know that. And, in their heart of hearts, they also know that a law perceived as unjust, a law routinely violated, can over time breed disrespect for law in general.

Slowly but surely we may be seeing a change in attitude. This summer, Dr. Morris Chafetz, a distinguished psychiatrist, a member of the presidential commission that recommended raising the drinking age, and the founder of the National Institute for Alcoholism and Alcohol Abuse admitted that supporting the higher drinking age is "the most regrettable decision of my entire professional career." This remarkable statement did not receive the attention it merited.

Alcohol is a reality in the lives of young adults. We can either try to change the reality—which has been our principal focus since 1984, by imposing Prohibition on young adults 18 to 20—or we can create the safest possible environment for the reality.

A drinking age minimum of 21 has not changed the reality. It's time to try something different.

It's not 1984 anymore.

| "It does not make sense to increase access to alcohol when there are already so many problems with underage drinking."

The Drinking Age Should Not Be Lowered

Misty Moyse and Melanie Fonder

Mothers Against Drunk Driving (MADD) was founded in 1980 to combat drunk driving both by raising awareness of the risks involved in driving while under the influence of alcohol and by lobbying for stricter laws regarding alcohol consumption (including the 1984 National Minimum Drinking Age Act, which required all fifty states to raise their drinking age to twenty-one as a condition of receiving federal highway funding). In the following viewpoint the authors argue that the current national minimum drinking age of twenty-one is "one of the nation's most scrutinized laws," and that it has, without a doubt, decreased drunk driving, underage drinking, and binge drinking.

As you read, consider the following questions:

1. How many lives does the U.S. Department of Transportation estimate are saved every year by the existence of a minimum drinking age of twenty-one?

2. According to a survey by the Nationwide Insurance company, what percentage of adults support a minimum drinking age of twenty-one? What percentage of adults believe lowering the drinking age would result in alcohol being more accessible to youths?

3. What percentage of college students abuse alcohol, and what percentage of college students are alcohol-dependent?

As students head back to school, more than 100 college and university presidents have signed on to a misguided initiative that uses deliberately misleading information to confuse the public on the effectiveness of the 21 law [setting the minimum drinking age at 21]. The initiative is led by another organization with a political agenda of lowering the drinking age in the name of reducing college binge drinking.

Mothers Against Drunk Driving (MADD) National President Laura Dean-Mooney said, "Underage and binge drinking is a tough problem and we welcome an honest discussion about how to address this challenge, but that discussion must honor the science behind the 21 law which unequivocally shows that the 21 law has reduced drunk driving and underage and binge drinking."

MADD, the Insurance Institute for Highway Safety (IIHS), the American Medical Association (AMA), National Transportation Safety Board (NTSB), Governors Highway Safety Association and other science, medical and public health organizations, and all members of the Support 21 Coalition call on these college and university presidents to remove their names from this list and urge them to work with the public health community and law enforcement on real solutions to underage and binge drinking. Additionally, MADD is asking the public to write letters to their governors and college presidents to support the 21 law and ask those on the initiative list to remove their names.

"As the mother of a daughter who is close to entering college, it is deeply disappointing to me that many of our educational leaders would support an initiative without doing their homework on the underlying research and science," said Dean-Mooney. "Parents should think twice before sending their teens to these colleges or any others that have waved the white flag on underage and binge drinking policies."

Politicians Support the Current Maximum Drinking Age

Top science, medical and public health experts as well as congressional and state leaders agree on the effectiveness of the 21 minimum drinking age law in saving lives.

University of Miami President and former U.S. Department of Health and Human Services Secretary Donna Shalala, said maintaining the legal drinking age at 21 is a socially and medically sound policy that helps parents, schools and law enforcement protect our youth from the potentially life-threatening effects of underage drinking. "As a three-time university president, I can tell you that losing a student to an alcohol-related tragedy is one of the hardest and most heart-rending experiences imaginable," Shalala said. "Signing this initiative does serious harm to the education and enforcement efforts on our campuses and ultimately endangers young lives even more. I ask every higher education leader who has signed to reconsider. I am old enough to remember life on our campuses before the [age] 21 . . . drinking rule. It was horrible."

"The traffic safety and public health benefits of the 21 minimum drinking age law have been well established, with the Department of Transportation estimating nearly 1,000 lives saved each year as a result. I strongly support this lifesaving law, and will not consider any effort to repeal or weaken it in any way," said Congressman James L. Oberstar (D-MN), Chairman, U.S. House Committee on Transportation and Infrastructure.

"Drunk driving needlessly kills thousands of young people every year. That's why I wrote a law to create a national drinking age of 21 and why we fight so hard to reduce drunk driving and save lives on our roads," Senator Frank R. Lautenberg (D-NJ) said. "This small minority of college administrators wants to undo years of success—that defies common sense. We need to do all we can to protect the national drinking age—a law that saves the lives of drivers, passengers and pedestrians across the country each year."

"Countless lives have been saved since Congress raised the national minimum drinking age to 21 in 1984. We need to maintain this important law and the life-saving protection it gives our teens and others on the roads," said U.S. Senator David Vitter (R-LA), a member of the Subcommittee on Transportation and Infrastructure of the U.S. Senate committee on Environment & Public Works.

Industry Experts Support the Current Law

Ronald M. Davis, Immediate Past President of the AMA said, "It is impossible to ignore the scientific evidence demonstrating the dangers of underage drinking. A young adult's brain is a work in progress, marked by significant development in areas of the brain responsible for learning, memory, complex thinking, planning, inhibition and emotional regulation. If we lower the age at which young adults are legally allowed to purchase alcohol, we are lowering the age of those who have easy access to alcohol and shifting responsibility to high school educators. The science simply does not support lowering the drinking age."

"Age 21 drinking laws are effective in preventing deaths and injuries," said NTSB Acting Chairman Mark V. Rosenker. "Repealing them is a terrible idea. It would be a national tragedy to turn back the clock and jeopardize the lives of more teens."

Adrian Lund, president of IIHS, said, "This initiative aims to lower the drinking age without proposing a realistic substitute. It reflects ignorance about the years of research comprising the scientific justification for 21 laws. Sound policy should be based on sound science. What is the evidence that education programs would be an effective replacement for minimum drinking age laws? There is none. If states lower the drinking age again, more teens will drink and drive and more will die."

The Law Has Both Public and Scientific Support

The public strongly disagrees with efforts to lower the drinking age. According to a new survey released today [August 19, 2008] by Nationwide Insurance, 78 percent of adults support 21 as the minimum drinking age and 72 percent believe lowering the drinking age would make alcohol more accessible to youth.

"While advocates argue a lower drinking age will curb teen binge drinking, our survey shows only 14 percent of Americans agree and 47 percent believe it will actually make a huge problem worse," said Bill Windsor, associate vice president of safety for Nationwide. "Americans feel so strongly about teen binge drinking [that] more than half say they are less likely to vote for a politician who supports lowering the legal limit or to send their child to a known 'party school.'"

As one of the most studied public health laws in history, the scientific research from more than 50 high-quality studies all found that the 21 law saves lives. In addition, studies show that the 21 law causes those under the age of 21 to drink less

"Excuse me, miss—are you spewing your guts up responsibly?" cartoon by Tom Williams. www.CartoonStock.com.

and to continue to drink less throughout their 20s. The earlier [that] youth drink (average age of first drink is about 16), the more likely they will become dependent on alcohol and drive drunk later in life.

Colleges Seen to Be Part of the Problem

There is a perfect storm of affluence, opportunity and tolerance on college campuses. Access to alcohol on college campuses is a particular problem—where underage students drink because they can and they are in a high-risk environment where enforcement of the law varies widely.

In fact, research shows that more than 30 percent of college students abuse alcohol and six percent are dependent on alcohol—rates much higher than for young adults who are not in college. Research also shows that the problem of binge drinking is worse among college-age students in college versus those who are not in college.

"By signing onto this initiative, these presidents have made the 21 law nearly unenforceable on their campuses. In fact, I call into question whether or not these campuses are bothering to enforce the 21 drinking age," said Dean-Mooney.

College Communities Can Be Part of the Solution

Some universities are taking strong steps to enforce the 21 law and change the drinking culture in their campus communities. Solutions to the problem are centered on enforcement of the 21 law, sanctions for adults providing alcohol to those under 21, changing the environment found on many college campuses and tightening alcohol policies on campuses, and working with local establishments in college communities selling alcohol to sell responsibly and to ensure those under 21 are not being served.

The U.S. Surgeon General issued a call to action to solve the underage and college binge drinking problem in 2007. Several steps have been taken by communities, and MADD will engage parents and other health and safety leaders this fall on the topic to ensure parents specifically are armed with the tools they need to combat underage drinking early—before peer pressure begins.

Dean-Mooney added, "It does not make sense to increase access to alcohol when there are already so many problems with underage drinking. As it stands, about 5,000 people under age 21 die each year due to underage drinking. This is not to mention the sexual assaults, violence, and injuries."

| "Compared with those who consumed their first alcohol drink after age 13 to 15 years, early-onset drinkers appeared to be more genetically susceptible to later [alcohol dependence] problems."

Early Drinking Leads to Alcohol Dependence

Ecology, Environment & Conservation Business Staff

The following viewpoint describes research and findings reported by Arpana Agrawal (assistant professor of psychiatry at Washington University School of Medicine) and Carol A. Prescott (professor of psychology at the University of Southern California). Agrawal's research was ultimately published in the journal Alcoholism: Clinical and Experimental Research *as "Evidence for an Interaction Between Age at First Drink and Genetic Influences on DSM-IV Alcohol Dependence Symptoms." Agrawal specifically found that it appeared likely that early experimentation with alcohol may actually activate genes that predispose an individual to ultimately develop a physiological dependence on alcohol.*

As you read, consider the following questions:

1. Describe the sample used by the researchers as precisely as possible.

2. According to the researchers, how many separate studies have linked early experimentation with alcohol to ultimately developing an alcohol dependence?

3. Can the researchers be sure that their findings are universal? Why or why not?

People who begin drinking at an early age are more likely to subsequently develop alcohol dependence (AD). A new study has found that age at first drink (AFD) may enhance the role of genetic factors that are already associated with vulnerability to AD symptoms. Heritable influences on AD symptoms were considerably greater in those who reported an AFD younger than 15 years of age.

Early Drinking Activates Alcohol-Dependence Genes

Individuals who begin drinking at an early age are more likely to subsequently develop alcohol dependence (AD). While age at first drink (AFD) and AD are influenced by similar genetic and environmental factors, AFD may also have an impact on the risk for AD. A new study has found that AFD may facilitate the expression of genes that are already associated with vulnerability to AD symptoms. . . .

"Drinking at an early age may create an environment where individuals can more easily transition from normative to problematic drinking," said Arpana Agrawal, assistant professor of psychiatry at Washington University School of Medicine and corresponding author for the study. "Early AFD is often part of other precocious/non-normative behaviors such as conduct problems, experimentation with drugs, and deviant peers. From a biological perspective, early AFD may induce changes in the highly sensitive adolescent brain, which may also modify an individual's subsequent genetic vulnerability to AD."

"This would mean that, for someone who is vulnerable, an experience or exposure leads to the expression of their preexisting risk to develop AD," added Carol A. Prescott, professor of psychology at the University of Southern California. "AFD could be said to have moderating effects if early alcohol exposure alters the trajectory an adolescent is on, for example, if early involvement then led to changes in academic achievement or peer group composition in ways that increased risk for later development of AD."

A Clear Link Between Early Drinking and Alcohol Dependence

Agrawal and her colleagues examined previously collected data on 6,257 adult, identical and fraternal, male and female Australian twins. They statistically examined the extent to which: AFD increased AD symptoms, and whether the magnitude of additive genetic, shared, and non-shared environmental influences on AD symptoms varied as a function of a lower AFD.

"In this sample of young adults of Caucasian ancestry from Australia, earlier AFD was associated with increased likelihood of a lifetime history of onset of AD symptoms, and with reporting more AD symptoms. It was also associated with increased genetic vulnerability to AD symptoms," said Agrawal. "Compared with those who consumed their first alcohol drink after age 13 to 15 years, early-onset drinkers appeared to be more genetically susceptible to later AD problems."

"These results may be interpreted in two ways," said Prescott. "Early drinking changes the course an individual is on, and is thus a direct cause of increased AD risk; and early drinking is correlated with AD risk, and is thus an indirect in-

One Million Hard-Drinking High Schoolers

The Centers for Disease Control and Prevention's 2003 Youth Risk Behavior Survey of high school students nationwide revealed that 28% drank alcohol other than a few sips before age 13 years. By age 17 years they were 7 times more likely to consume 5 or more drinks 6 or more times per month than those who waited until they were 17 years or older to begin drinking. The National Institute on Alcohol Abuse and Alcoholism has defined binge drinking as males consuming 5 or more and females 4 or more drinks in 2 hours. Binge drinking for the average person on an empty stomach produces a blood alcohol level of 0.08% or higher, the legal level of intoxication in every state. Thus, those who begin drinking before age 13 years are much more likely even in high school to frequently drink to intoxication. Compared with other students, the approximately 1 million frequent heavy drinkers more often exhibit behaviors that pose risk to themselves and others, such as riding with drinking drivers; driving after drinking; never wearing safety belts; carrying guns and other weapons; becoming injured in fights and suicide attempts; having unplanned and unprotected sex; becoming or making someone else pregnant; using tobacco, marijuana, and other illicit drugs; drinking and smoking marijuana at school; and earning mostly low grades (*D*'s and *F*'s) in school.

Ralph W. Hingson, Timothy Heeren, and Michael R. Winter,
"Age at Drinking Onset & Alcohol Dependence,"
Archives of Pediatrics & Adolescent Medicine, *July 2006.*

dicator of AD risk. The results from this study suggest that both explanations are partially correct."

Agrawal believes it is possible that use of alcohol at a particularly early age may lead to modifications in the developing brain, which, in turn, may modify expression of AD-related genes. "However," she added, "it is equally likely that a set of common genes contribute to the likelihood of early AFD and AD."

Looking for Genes

Neither Agrawal nor Prescott were surprised that heritable influences on AD symptoms were considerably greater in those who reported an AFD of younger than 15 years of age. "At least 12 studies from several different countries have found that individuals whose (genetic or environmental) predispositions lead them to try alcohol at an earlier age have greater risk to develop alcohol-related problems," said Prescott.

"Additionally," said Agrawal, "we found that in individuals who began drinking at a later age, genetic influences played a much smaller part and that non-shared environment gained prominence. This suggests that AD problems in those with later AFD, while less common, are attributable to unique experiences of those individuals, for example, a traumatic life event."

Agrawal noted that these findings have implications for future research. "From a gene-finding standpoint, which is now gaining even more momentum, we urge scientists to consider the role of AFD," she said. "Our work and that of others suggests heterogeneity [diversity] in the role of genes acting on AD risk as a consequence of early or late AFD."

Impacts on Public Health Strategies

These findings also have public-health and education implications, particularly for "tweens" and teens, about problems associated with early drinking. "We show that even though there are common, underlying risk and protective factors for AFD and AD," said Agrawal, "encouraging youth to initiate drinking alcohol at a later age may reduce the likelihood of expression of genetic vulnerability to later alcohol problems. This does not imply that later-onset drinkers will never develop AD, but their risk seems largely attributable to individual environmental experiences."

Given that this study is based on a sample of twins from Australia, as noted by Prescott, which has a different drinking culture and practices than in the U.S., Agrawal and her colleagues will next try to replicate these findings in other older and younger Australian and U.S. samples to see if these findings are unique to this group of young adult Australians or more general in nature.

> *"Many studies have focused on the rates of alcohol and drug use and abuse among children of alcoholics, and most have similarly concluded that this population is significantly more vulnerable to substance abuse problems."*

Children of Alcoholics Are More Likely to Abuse Substances

Diana Mahoney

Diana Mahoney regularly writes for Clinical Psychiatry News, *a leading monthly publication reporting on developments in psychiatry. The following viewpoint reports that, based on a large number of studies, the children of alcoholics are more likely to experiment with drugs and alcohol, do so earlier in life, develop drug and alcohol problems more swiftly, and struggle with these problems later into adulthood. The author goes on to argue that, because there are common traits among the children of alcoholics who do not develop such substance abuse problems as their parents experienced, intervention programs should work to foster these common characteristics of "resilient" children.*

As you read, consider the following questions:

1. By age seventeen, what percentage of the children of alcoholics had smoked cigarettes or marijuana, or drank alcohol? What percentage of the children of nonalcoholics had done so?

2. By what age are most individuals expected to have "matured out of drug use"?

3. What are the four characteristics shared by all of the "resilient" children in Emmy Werner's Kauai longitudinal study?

The legacy of parental alcoholism cuts deep. Nearly 6.2 million children in the United States younger than 18 years old live with at least one parent who is currently [in 2009] dependent on alcohol, according to estimates from the 1996 National Household Survey on Drug Abuse (NHSDA, now known as the National Survey on Drug Use and Health). The number increases exponentially when it is broadened to include those children living with adults who have abused or been dependent on alcohol [at] some time in their lives.

The Children of Alcoholics Use Drugs Earlier and at Higher Rates

Research has long established that having an alcoholic parent increases a child's risk for multiple negative behavioral and developmental outcomes. That increased risk is conveyed through social, emotional, environmental, and biologic pathways. In particular, many studies have focused on the rates of alcohol and drug use and abuse among children of alcoholics, and most [researchers] have similarly concluded that this population is significantly more vulnerable to substance abuse problems than their peers from nonalcoholic families.

Data from a national epidemiologic survey out of Johns Hopkins University, Baltimore, for example, show that children of a parent with active alcohol dependence initiated use of alcohol, cigarettes, and marijuana earlier and at higher age-specific rates than children who did not have an alcohol-dependent parent.

Using NHSDA information collected from 1995 to 1997, the investigators identified a sample of 2,888 parent-child pairs, which included 114 children of alcohol-dependent parents and 2,774 children whose interviewed parent was not dependent on alcohol. The odds ratios for past-year tobacco, alcohol, and marijuana use for the children with alcoholic parents were 3.2, 1.6, and 2.9, respectively.

The differences in substance use between the two groups started to emerge as early as age 9 years, and the additional risk was sustained at least through age 17 years, the authors wrote. By 17 years, 73% the children of alcoholic parents had smoked cigarettes, 70% had begun drinking alcohol, and 41% had smoked marijuana, compared with 44%, 57%, and 26%, respectively, of the children from nonalcoholic homes.

The Children of Alcoholics Develop Drug Problems More Quickly

In addition to an increased risk for substance use in this population, there also appears to be a greater likelihood of an accelerated trajectory from onset of drinking and drug use to problem substance use, a recent study by Andrea Hussong, Ph.D., of the University of North Carolina, Chapel Hill, and her colleagues shows. Using longitudinal data from a community-based sample, the investigators conducted survival analyses and determined that children of alcoholics progressed more quickly from initial adolescent alcohol use to the onset of disorder than matched controls, even after controlling for externalizing symptoms and heavier drinking patterns at initiation. A similar "telescoping" risk was observed for drug disorders.

With respect to illicit drug use, adolescent children of alcoholics who use drugs are more likely to continue doing so during their transition to young adulthood than their peers from non-alcoholic families. In a study that tracked and monitored the drug use habits of 545 adolescent children of alcoholics and demographically matched children of nonalcoholic parents for 15 years, David B. Flora, Ph.D., of the University of North Carolina, Chapel Hill, and his colleagues determined that the control group significantly decreased their drug use during this time, consistent with national data, while the children of alcoholics did not.

The findings show that "[children of alcoholics] do not typically follow the normative trend by which individuals are expected to mature out of drug use before age 30," the authors wrote.

The investigators also looked at the impact of marriage on drug use trajectories in young adult children of alcoholics and determined that "marriage mediated but did not moderate the relations between parental alcoholism and the rate of change in drug use during the transition into young adulthood and the level of drug use at ages 25 to 30."

Although marriage predicted the amount of drug use in men 25–30 years old—about 94% of married men either remained abstinent from drugs or decreased their drug use—the children of alcoholics in this study were less likely to be married and thus not only had smaller decreases in drug use between 25 and 30, they had higher levels of drug use overall, according to the authors.

Resilience Among the Children of Alcoholics

In addition to a proclivity [attraction to] for alcohol and drug use and abuse, children of alcoholics are at increased risk for other negative outcomes, including conduct problems, aggression, depression, and anxiety, according to the Substance Abuse and Mental Health Services Administration (SAMHSA).

But not all children of alcoholics succumb to the potential negative consequences. In fact, studies suggest that, despite the odds, a large proportion of children of alcoholics do not develop serious problems.

In an often-cited longitudinal study of children of alcoholics born on the Hawaiian island of Kauai, psychologist Emmy Werner, Ph.D., of the University of California, Davis, reported on 49 children of alcoholic parents who were raised in chronic poverty from birth to 18 years. Although 41% of the study participants had developed coping problems by age 18, 59% appeared to cope well and had not developed serious problems. Among the shared characteristics of the "resilient" children were adequate communication skills, average intelligence, a desire to achieve, and the ability to get positive attention from other people.

A later report on the same cohort [group] showed that study participants who effectively coped with the trauma of growing up with an alcoholic parent and became competent adults by age 32 had relied on more sources of support in their childhood than did those offspring of alcoholics with coping problems.

In a separate 3-year study of 267 adolescents, including 127 children of alcoholics, self-awareness, a perceived control over one's environment, and the possession of cognitive coping skills were all identified as having a buffering effect against potential negative consequences associated with having an alcoholic parent.

Building Resilience Is an Important Community Health Goal

Although resilience in children of alcoholics is still not fully understood—a recent study by the University of Michigan, Ann Arbor, that has identified differences in neural activation mechanisms between vulnerable and resilient children of alcoholic parents adds a new dimension to the research in this arena—the available evidence suggests that building resilience is a critical intervention goal.

For example, in a school-based prevention intervention called Students Together and Resourceful (STAR)—identified as a model program by SAMHSA—children of alcoholics gain self-efficacy through education about alcoholism and its effects on the family as well as group exercises that allow participants to recognize and express their feelings and to practice problem-solving, stress-management, and alcohol-refusal skills. In randomized trials comparing outcomes of children of alcoholics who did and did not participate in the intervention, participants attained improved self-concept as well as decreases in depression.

Certain elements of the STAR program should be universal to all interventions for this population, according to lead author James Emshoff, Ph.D., professor of psychology at Georgia State University, Atlanta. These include "skill building in the areas of coping and social competence, social support, an outlet for the safe expression of feelings, and healthy alternative activities."

Periodical Bibliography

The following articles have been selected to supplement the diverse views presented in this chapter.

Geoffrey C. Cook
"Good Reasons to Keep Drinking Age at 21," *Daily Messenger* (Canandaigua, NY), November 23, 2009.

Robert A. Corrigan
"Keep the Drinking Age at 21," *San Francisco Chronicle*, August 29, 2008.

David J. Hanson
"Early Onset of Drinking: What Research Says & What Anti-Alcohol Activists Say It Says," October 24, 2009. www2.potsdam.edu.

David J. Hanson
"Binge Drinking," January 13, 2010. www2.potsdam.edu/hansondj/BingeDrinking.html.

New York Times
"Binge Drinking on Campus," June 30, 2009.

David Oxtoby
"Opposing View: Law Makes Matters Worse," *USA Today*, August 27, 2008.

Heidi Splete
"Complex Factors Drive Underage Alcohol Use," *Clinical Psychiatry News*, June 2008.

John Stossel
"The Drinking Age Myth," September 3, 2008. http://townhall.com.

Alex Torpey
"Proposal for Graduated Alcohol Policies," White House 2, July 6, 2009. www.whitehouse2.org.

Washington Post
"A Lower Drinking Age?" July 12, 2009.

What Are the Causes and Effects of Teen Substance Abuse?

Chapter Preface

A lthough the University of Michigan Monitoring the Future survey, which tracks adolescent drug use, makes clear that rates of teen drug use are holding steady (or even declining) in the United States, it is nonetheless also clear that those teens who do abuse drugs often suffer a wide range of other problems: unwanted pregnancy, medical issues, psychological disorders, criminal victimization, and being prosecuted for crimes they themselves commit. While conventional wisdom holds that drugs and drug addiction are to blame, the research is far from clear: Does drug abuse make teens into delinquents, or do teens with existing psycho-emotional problems, socio-economic challenges, or criminal tendencies gravitate toward drug use?

A 2008 report released by the ONDCP (the Office of National Drug Control Policy, often referred to as the nation's "drug czar") announced that new research demonstrated a clear causal relationship between marijuana use and depression, with strong indications that prolonged marijuana use lead to schizophrenia and other psychosis. While the findings of the ONDCP report were widely repeated in news media without commentary or criticism, there was no actual scientific consensus on the links between marijuana use and psychoses at that time (nor is there today). Just days before the ONDCP released its report, Britain's Advisory Panel on the Misuse of Drugs officially determined, after years of consideration, that "the evidence for the existence of an association between frequency of cannabis use and the development of psychosis is, on the available evidence, weak." This followed a well-received report published in the prestigious British medical journal *The Lancet*, which noted that "projected trends for schizophrenia incidence have not paralleled trends in cannabis use over time," making it highly unlikely that marijuana use—in and of itself, without complicating factors or preexisting conditions—can cause such severe mental disorders. In fact, several studies have shown a tendency among adolescents already suffering from depression or emerging psychoses to "self-medicate" with marijuana, although researchers are undecided as to whether such use worsens the existing disorder, helps the sufferer cope with the symptoms (and thus avoid treatment until the condition is much worse), or has little real impact on the underlying problem.

Nonetheless, NORML—the National Organization for the Reform of Marijuana Laws, which seeks to "repeal cannabis prohibition" in the United States—publicly acknowledges that there is some reliable data showing an association between chronic marijuana use and the development of psychoses in those predisposed to mental illness.

The authors of the following viewpoints explore both the causes and effects of teen drug abuse, and they attempt to clarify which is which.

| *"Recent research makes a strong case that cannabis smoking itself may be a causal agent in psychiatric symptoms."*

Marijuana Use Worsens Teen Depression

Office of National Drug Control Policy

The Office of National Drug Control Policy (ONDCP) was established as a part of the 1988 Anti-Drug Abuse Act. The primary purpose of the ONDCP is to reduce or eliminate illicit drug manufacture, trafficking, and use, as well as drug-related crime and health issues. The following viewpoint is drawn from the ONDCP's 2008 report Teen Marijuana Use Worsens Depression. *Here the authors argue that, based on an array of studies published since 1998, there are strong indications that marijuana use coincides with, and quite likely causes, serious psychological problems, including depression, anxiety, schizophrenia, and other psychoses.*

As you read, consider the following questions:

1. How much more likely is a depressed teen to use marijuana than a nondepressed teen?

Teen Marijuana Use Worsens Depression: An Analysis of Recent Data Shows "Self-Medicating" Could Actually Make Things Worse, Office of National Drug Control Policy, 2008.

2. According to one sixteen-year study, how much more likely are nondepressed people to develop depression after using marijuana?

3. During a given year, how many more teen girls experience depression than boys?

Millions of American teens [ages 12–17] report experiencing weeks of hopelessness and loss of interest in normal daily activities, and many of these depressed teens are making the problem worse by using marijuana and other drugs. Some teens use marijuana to relieve the symptoms of depression ("self-medicate"), wrongly believing it may alleviate these depressed feelings. In surveys, teens often report using marijuana and other drugs not only to relieve symptoms of depression, but also to "feel good," or "feel better," to relieve stress, and help them cope.

"Self-Medicating" Can Actually Make Psychological Problems Worse

However, recent studies show that marijuana and depression are a dangerous combination. In fact, using marijuana can *worsen depression* and lead to more serious mental health disorders, such as schizophrenia, anxiety, and even suicide. Weekly or more frequent use of marijuana *doubles* a teen's risk of depression and anxiety. Depressed teens are more than *twice as likely* as their peers to abuse or become dependent on marijuana.

Alarmingly, the majority of teens who report feeling depressed aren't getting professional help. They have not seen or spoken to a medical doctor or other professional about their feelings. For parents, this means they need to pay closer attention to their teen's behavior and mood swings, and recognize that marijuana and other drugs could be playing a dangerous role in their child's life.

According to recent national surveys, two million youths (8%) felt depressed at some point in the course of a year. Another survey of high school students shows that percentage even higher (29%).

There are indications that many teens are using drugs to "self-medicate" (deal with problems of depression and anxiety by using drugs to alleviate the symptoms). Many teens say they use drugs to "make them feel good" or "feel better."

However, research shows that using marijuana and other illicit drugs puts a teen at even greater risk for more serious mental illnesses. A teen who has been depressed at some point in the past year is more than *twice as likely* to have used marijuana (25%) as teens who have not reported being depressed (12%). Similarly, 35 percent of depressed teens used an illicit drug (including marijuana) during the year, compared to 18 percent of teens who did not report being depressed.

Depressed teens are more likely to engage in other risky behaviors, as well. They are more likely than non-depressed teens to report daily cigarette use (5% vs. 3%) and heavy alcohol use (5% vs. 2%).

A Strong Link Between Marijuana and Psychosis

Teens who use marijuana can end up making tough times worse. Mental health risks associated with recent and long-term marijuana use include schizophrenia, other forms of psychosis, and even suicide. Recent research makes a strong case that cannabis smoking itself may be a causal agent in psychiatric symptoms, particularly schizophrenia.

Research shows that teens who smoke marijuana at least once a month in the past year are three times more likely to have suicidal thoughts than non-users during the same period. Yet another study found that marijuana use was associated with depression, suicidal thoughts, and suicide attempts.

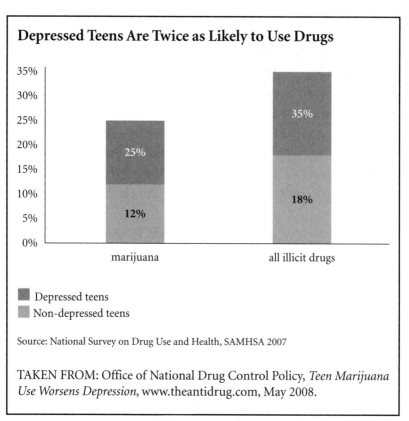

Depressed Teens Are Twice as Likely to Use Drugs

Depressed teens
Non-depressed teens

Source: National Survey on Drug Use and Health, SAMHSA 2007

TAKEN FROM: Office of National Drug Control Policy, *Teen Marijuana Use Worsens Depression*, www.theantidrug.com, May 2008.

One 16-year study showed that individuals who were not depressed and then used marijuana were four times more likely to be depressed at follow up. Another study conducted over a 14-year period found that marijuana use was a predictor of later major depressive disorder.

An extensive analysis of longitudinal studies on marijuana use and risk of mental illness later in life showed that marijuana use increases the risk of developing mental disorders by 40 percent. The risk of psychosis increases with frequency of marijuana use, from 50 to 200 percent among frequent users. The authors conclude that "there is now sufficient evidence to warn young people that using cannabis could increase their risk of developing a psychotic illness later in life."

Marijuana and Schizophrenia

Other studies also show a strong relationship between marijuana and schizophrenia. A study from New Zealand showed "a clear increase in rates of psychotic symptoms after the start of regular use" of marijuana. Another 21-year longitudinal study showed that marijuana use was associated with psychotic symptoms and suggested a causal relationship. A study published in *Schizophrenia Research* found that cannabis use seems to be a specific risk factor for future psychotic symptoms.

Another study of young adults from birth to age 21 found a relationship between early initiation and frequent use of cannabis and symptoms of anxiety and depression, regardless of a history of mental illness.

Teens who smoke marijuana when feeling depressed are also more likely to become addicted to marijuana or other illicit drugs. Eight percent of depressed teens abused or became dependent on marijuana during the year they experienced depression, compared with only three percent of non-depressed teens. Overall, more teens are in treatment for marijuana dependence than for any other illicit drug.

Teens, Especially Girls, More Likely to Self-Medicate than Adults

The percentage of teens reporting being depressed is similar to the percentage of adults reporting depression. Depressed teens, however, are more likely than depressed adults to use drugs. In the course of a year, seven percent of adults reported feeling depressed, compared to eight percent of teens.

But a quarter (25%) of depressed teens used marijuana in the course of a year, while only 19 percent of depressed adults did. Additionally, 35 percent of depressed teens used other illicit drugs (including marijuana), compared to 28 percent of depressed adults.

Teen girls are especially at risk. In fact, three times as many girls (12%) as boys (4%) experienced depression during the year. Another study confirms that girls are more likely than boys to report feelings of sadness or hopelessness (37% vs. 29%).

Substance abuse can compound the problem. Girls who smoke marijuana daily are significantly more likely to develop symptoms of depression and anxiety: Their odds are more than five times higher than those of girls who do not smoke marijuana.

Parental Relationships Make a Difference

Parents should not dismiss changes in their teen's behavior as a "phase." Their teen could be depressed, using drugs—or both. Parents can help their teen understand the risks of marijuana use and should be on the lookout for signs of depression.

It's been shown that parents who make an effort to understand the pressures and influences on young people are more likely to keep their teen healthy and drug-free.

Teens who report having conversations with their parents about alcohol and drug use are more likely to stay drug-free, compared to teens who do not talk about substance abuse with their parents.

| *"Patient reports and observations, backed by known pharmacology, suggest that . . . cannabis derivatives . . . may have mood-stabilizing properties."*

Alcohol, Not Marijuana, Worsens Depression

Marijuana Policy Project

The Marijuana Policy Project is dedicated to minimizing the harm associated with marijuana by supporting "non-punitive, non-coercive marijuana policies." The following viewpoint is drawn from their Summer 2005 Marijuana Policy Report *newsletter and argues that the Office of National Drug Control Policy's position that marijuana "causes" psychoses relies on a small number of studies while ignoring a much larger body of evidence, some of which indicates that the active chemicals in marijuana may have a moderating effect on mental disorders. While the connection between marijuana and depression is dubious, there is incontrovertible evidence that alcohol abuse—even among adults—deepens depression and contributes to suicide.*

"Marijuana, Mental Illness, and Government Disinformation," *Marijuana Policy Report*, vol. 11, issue 2, Summer 2005, pp. 10–11. Copyright © 2006 Marijuana Policy Project. All rights reserved. Reproduced by permission.

As you read, consider the following questions:

1. How long do THC metabolites persist in a marijuana smoker's body?

2. How much greater is the risk that an alcohol abuser will complete suicide, compared to a nonabuser of alcohol?

3. Do several studies (including one by Dutch researchers and published in *Addiction*, the other by a U.S. team, published in *Psychiatry Research*) suggest that psychotic symptoms precede or follow marijuana use?

This spring [2005], the federal government embarked on a new campaign to frighten Americans into believing that marijuana use—particularly by teens—causes serious mental illness, including schizophrenia, depression, and suicide. White House Drug Czar John Walters [retired January 20, 2009] and his fellow prohibitionists made their case by cherry-picking data that seemed to support their argument, ignoring studies that contradicted it, and even putting out a misleading account of a teenage boy's suicide—exploiting the boy's grieving parents in the process.

A Tragedy Erroneously Attributed to Marijuana

"A growing body of evidence now demonstrates that smoking marijuana can increase the risk of serious mental health problems," Walters said at a May 3 [2005] news conference, providing reporters with a list of studies allegedly making such a connection. The emotional centerpiece of the event was the story of 15-year-old Christopher Skaggs, told by his parents. Mrs. Skaggs described how her son was caught smoking marijuana in January 2004 and committed suicide seven months later. The media were encouraged to report that his death resulted from use of "this very dangerous drug."

But later that week, in an interview on the Peter Boyles Show on KHOW-AM in Denver, Mrs. Skaggs revealed that toxicology tests run on Christopher in the hospital before he was pronounced dead found "nothing in his system but alcohol at that time." And in the four separate drug tests done between January and July [2004], no traces of marijuana were ever found. On the other hand, Christopher was known to have been using alcohol—a known risk factor for depression—at about the same time he was caught smoking marijuana. None of this had been explained to the media.

Because metabolites from THC (the primary psychoactive chemical in marijuana) can be detected for days after marijuana use—and for as long as 30 days in regular smokers—the series of negative tests indicates not only that Christopher was not under the influence of marijuana when he killed himself, but also that he almost certainly was not a regular smoker during the months prior to his death. He was, however, incontrovertibly under the influence of alcohol when he killed himself.

A Strong Connection Between Alcohol and Suicide

The scientific evidence implicating alcohol as a risk factor for depression and suicide is overwhelming. Alcohol intoxication increases reckless and impulsive behavior, and a review of 42 studies published in December 2004 in the journal *Drug and Alcohol Dependence* found that alcohol abusers are at 979% greater risk for completing suicide than people who are not alcohol abusers. A Columbia University study of nearly 1,500 teens published in the Winter 2004 issue of *Suicide and Life-Threatening Behavior* reported, "Alcohol abuse and dependence appeared to be strongly associated with suicide attempts," while researchers found no such relationship involving the abuse of illicit drugs, including marijuana. "The relationship between alcohol and suicidality may involve the disinhibitory effects of acute alcohol intoxication" as well as "the increase in vulnerability to depression," they wrote.

In contrast, the evidence linking marijuana use to adolescent depression and suicide consists almost entirely of "associations"—that is, kids who use marijuana tend, on average, to be more depressed than those who don't. But is marijuana making them depressed, or do depressed teens turn to marijuana as a way of escaping their problems? Existing data provide no definitive answer.

Marijuana Alleviates Depression

Or could it be that marijuana actually relieves depression? Several surveys of medical marijuana patients suffering from multiple sclerosis, ALS ("Lou Gehrig's disease"), or HIV/AIDS have reported relief from depression and improved mood as a major benefit from marijuana use. An article published this Spring [2005] in the *Journal of Psychopharmacology* suggests that cannabinoids may help treat bipolar disorder (sometimes called "manic depression"), of which depression is a significant component. "Patient reports and observations, backed by known pharmacology, suggest that the cannabis derivatives delta-9 tetrahydrocannabinol (THC) and cannabidiol (CBD) may have mood-stabilizing properties" the article notes, citing evidence that these marijuana components have anxiety-reducing, antidepressant, and antipsychotic effects.

Walters and his colleagues also linked marijuana use to psychosis, including schizophrenia, but again the real picture is far murkier than the cartoon version presented by the drug czar. It has long been known that some people with preexisting tendencies toward mental illness get worse if they use marijuana, but Walters suggested that marijuana makes normal people crazy, à la "Reefer Madness [a 1936 film depicting the horrors of Marijuana use]."

While there is some evidence suggesting that young marijuana users go on to develop symptoms of schizophrenia at higher rates than those who abstain, serious questions have been raised about these studies. For example, one much-hyped study published in the March [2005] issue of *Addiction* counted having "ideas or beliefs that others do not share" and "feeling other people cannot be trusted" as schizophrenia symptoms. But, as MPP's [Marijuana Policy Project's] Bruce Mirken and University of Southern California substance abuse researcher Dr. Mitch Earleywine pointed out in a letter to the journal, for a person using an illegal, socially frowned-upon substance, such beliefs are "not a sign of mental illness, but rather an indication of a rational, thinking person realistically assessing his or her situation."

And other recent research—including a Dutch study published in *Addiction* and a U.S. study published in *Psychiatry Research*—suggests that psychotic symptoms often come before marijuana use, not after.

Most importantly, periods when marijuana use increased markedly—such as the '60s and '70s—were not followed by increased rates of mental illness. As Dr. Earleywine has noted, this strongly suggests that if marijuana plays any role in inducing mental illness, it is likely weak, rare, or both.

> *"Evidence has recently emerged that some people's genetic make-up may predispose them to be particularly vulnerable to the effects of marijuana on mental health."*

There Is a Link Between Substance Abuse and Teen Suicide

PR Newswire

PR Newswire is a leading global vendor in information and news distribution services for professional communicators. In the following viewpoint, information presented from studies shows a link between teen drug use and suicide. John P. Walters and the Substance Abuse and Mental Health Services Administration (SAMHSA) alerted parents to the dangers of marijuana in relation to their teens' health.

As you read, consider the following questions:

1. According to the article, what can marijuana use—specifically during teen years—lead to?

2. What is a crucial risk factor in the later development of mental health issues according to this viewpoint?

3. Teens who smoke marijuana on a weekly basis are how many times more likely to have suicidal thoughts?

The Nation's Drug Czar, John P. Walters, and the Substance Abuse and Mental Health Services Administration (SAMHSA) Administrator, Charles G. Curie, joined with scientists and experts from the leading mental health organizations today to alert parents about the danger marijuana poses to their teens' mental health.

"A growing body of evidence now demonstrates that smoking marijuana can increase the risk of serious mental health problems," said Walters, director of National Drug Control Policy. "New research being conducted here and abroad illustrates that marijuana use, particularly during the teen years, can lead to depression, thoughts of suicide, and schizophrenia. This is yet another reason that parents must stay closely involved with their teens and ensure that they are not smoking marijuana."

Link Between Marijuana and Mental Health

A number of prominent studies have recently identified a direct link between marijuana use and increased risk of mental health problems. Recent research makes a stronger case that cannabis smoking itself is a causal agent in psychiatric symptoms, particularly schizophrenia. During the past three years, these studies have strengthened that association and further found that the age when marijuana is first smoked is a crucial risk factor in later development of mental health problems.

A report released today from SAMHSA found that adults who first used marijuana before age 12 were twice as likely as adults who first used marijuana at age 18 or older to be classified as having serious mental illness in the past year than were adults who first used marijuana at age 18 or older.

"Kids today are using marijuana at younger ages, putting them at greater risk," said Charles G. Curie, SAMHSA administrator. "We have found that the younger a person starts smoking marijuana, the greater the likelihood they have of developing an addiction and serious mental illness later in life."

"Mental health disorders such as depression and schizophrenia contribute to the mortality of our citizens, and suicide is one of the leading preventable causes of death," said U.S. Surgeon General Richard H. Carmona, M.D., M.P.H., F.A.C.S. "As a society we must do everything we can to promote mental health and prevent mental illness—and that includes keeping our kids drug-free. Parents and teens alike must realize the long-term effects marijuana can have on the brain."

Several recent studies have linked youth marijuana use with depression, suicidal thoughts and schizophrenia:

—Young people who use marijuana weekly have double the risk of developing depression.

—Teens aged 12 to 17 who smoke marijuana weekly are three times more likely than non-users to have suicidal thoughts.

—Marijuana use in some teens has been linked to increased risk for schizophrenia in later years.

—A British study found that as many as one in four people may have a genetic profile that makes marijuana five times more likely to trigger psychotic disorders.

Genetics and Marijuana

Evidence has recently emerged that some people's genetic make-up may predispose them to be particularly vulnerable to the effects of marijuana on mental health. For instance, a major study out of the Netherlands concluded that use of the drug "moderately increases" the risk of psychotic symptoms in young people but has "a much stronger effect" in those with evidence of predisposition.

"The nonchalance about marijuana in Europe and the U.S. is worrisome," said Neil McKeganey, Ph.D., professor of drug misuse research and director, Centre for Drug Misuse Research, University of Glasgow, Glasgow, Scotland. "Marijuana is the first illegal drug that many young people use and teens don't view it as a serious drug, and when children are exposed only to advice from kids like themselves, the risks seem meaningless. We're starting to see marijuana in a new light given recent research into the connection between marijuana and mental illness."

This new evidence comes with a warning to parents, as they are the most important influence in their teens' lives when it comes to drugs. "Tell your teens the facts and tell them not to use marijuana," said Robert L. DuPont, M.D., president of the Institute for Behavior and Health, Inc., and a leading advocate for the power of parents in preventing drug use. "Take meaningful actions to see that they do not. A vital part of your job as a parent is helping your teen grow up drug-free."

As part of the Office of National Drug Control Policy's (ONDCP) National Youth Anti-Drug Media Campaign, this outreach effort features a compendium of recent research linking marijuana and mental illness and an Open Letter to parents on "Marijuana and Your Teen's Mental Health." The letter highlights some of the new research about the serious consequences of teen marijuana use on mental health and is signed by ONDCP and 12 of the nation's leading mental health, behavioral health and addiction treatment organizations: American Psychiatric Association; American Academy of Child and Adolescent Psychiatry; American Society of Addiction Medicine; Asian Community Mental Health Services; Association for Medical Education and Research in Substance

Abuse; Institute for Behavior and Health, Inc.; National Asian American Pacific Islander Mental Health Association; National Association of Addiction Treatment Providers; National Council for Community Behavioral Healthcare; National Latino Behavioral Health Association; National Medical Association; and the Partnership for a Drug-Free America. The letter begins appearing next week [May 2005] in *USA Today* and newspapers in the 25 largest cities nationwide, including the *New York Times* and the *Washington Post*, and will run in *The Nation*, the *National Journal*, the *National Review*, the *New Republic*, *Newsweek*, *Time* and the *Weekly Standard*.

On the Media Campaign's Web site for parents, http://theantidrug.com, adults can learn more about how marijuana affects the developing teen brain, including the links between marijuana and depression, suicidal thoughts and schizophrenia. Visitors can take a virtual tour of a human brain to learn how marijuana impairs, and even changes, the functionality of the centers responsible for maintaining overall mental health. Parents can also view responses from a qualified psychiatrist on the most common questions regarding marijuana and mental health.

| *"This year's survey reveals a tight con-nection between teen sexual behavior and substance abuse."*

Teen Sex Is Linked to Drug Abuse

Richard Mulieri and Lauren Duran

The following viewpoint was released by the National Center on Addiction and Substance Abuse (also called CASA, since it was originally named the Center on Addiction and Substance Abuse), and is drawn from the press release issued following CASA's ninth annual National Survey of American Attitudes on Substance Abuse in 2004. At that time, CASA found a strong correlation between teen sexual experimentation (including watching pornography), drug and alcohol abuse, and smoking. Since its inception, CASA has promoted strong family engagement as a simple and effective way to prevent the likelihood of teen substance abuse.

Richard Mulieri and Lauren Duran, "Sexually Active Friends and Dating Practices Can Signal Increase In a Teen's Substance Abuse Risk: Girls Who Date Boys Two or More Years Older Likelier to Smoke, Drink, Get Drunk, and Use Illegal Drugs," *The National Center on Addiction and Substance Abuse at Columbia University, National Survey of American Attitudes on Substance Abuse IX: Teen Dating Practices and Sexual Activity,* August 19, 2004. Copyright © 2004 The National Center on Addiction and Substance Abuse at Columbia University. All rights reserved. Reproduced by permission.

As you read, consider the following questions:

1. How much likelier are teens with sexually active friends to drink, get drunk, try marijuana, or smoke cigarettes?

2. According to this survey, if a teen's friends regularly download pornography, how much likelier is that teen to smoke, drink, or use illegal drugs?

3. What percentage of teens twelve to seventeen report that they can get marijuana within one hour?

The more sexually active friends a teen has and the more time a teen spends with a boyfriend or girlfriend, the greater the risk that teen will smoke, drink, get drunk or use illegal drugs, according to the *National Survey of American Attitudes on Substance Abuse IX: Teen Dating Practices and Sexual Activity*, an annual back-to-school survey conducted by the National Center on Addiction and Substance Abuse (CASA) at Columbia University.

A Startling Link Between Sex and Drug Abuse

This ninth annual CASA survey found:

- Compared to teens with no sexually active friends, teens who report half or more of their friends are sexually active are more than six and one-half times likelier to drink; 31 times likelier to get drunk; 22.5 times likelier to have tried marijuana; and more than five and one-half times likelier to smoke.

- Teens who spend 25 or more hours a week with a boyfriend/girlfriend are two and one-half times likelier to drink; five times likelier to get drunk; four and one-half times likelier to have tried marijuana; and more than two and one-half times likelier to smoke than teens who spend less than 10 hours a week with a boyfriend/girlfriend.

Harvard Researchers Link Teen Substance Use and Body Modification

In one study among patients committed to a psychiatric institution, increasing sites and numbers of body modification were associated with more severe violent behavior. Among adolescent detainees, tattooing has been correlated with alcohol and drug use. An Australian study of amateur tattooing practices among high school students showed that students with tattoos had higher scores on school-related problem scales than those without tattoos. Recent [2001] data from the National Longitudinal Study of Adolescent Health demonstrated that tattooing was associated with sexual intercourse, substance use, violence, and truancy among teens. Additionally, body piercing was correlated with truancy among both male and female adolescents, and with sexual intercourse and smoking among female adolescents. Finally, a study of Australians aged over 14 years found that approximately 8% of those who had obtained body modification reported that they were under the influence of alcohol or other drugs while undergoing the procedure.

Because little is known about the range of body modification practices among adolescents, we sought to describe the prevalence and patterns of body modification in our adolescent clinic patient population. Substance use is a prevalent risk behavior in adolescents that may be associated with body modification because of clustering of risk behaviors. In addition, alcohol and drugs may impair judgment, resulting in a decision to obtain body modification, or they may be used for pain control during or after body modification procedures. We therefore hypothesized that adolescents who engage in body modification are more likely to report problem substance use than those who do not.

Traci L. Brooks, Elizabeth R. Woods, John R. Knight,
and Lydia A. Shrier, "Body Modification & Substance Use:
Is There a Link?" Journal of Adolescent Health, *January 2003.*

- Girls with boyfriends two or more years older are more than twice as likely to drink; almost six times likelier to get drunk; six times likelier to have tried marijuana; and four and one-half times likelier to smoke than girls whose boyfriends are less than two years older or who do not have a boyfriend.

"The message for parents from this year's survey is clear— the thunder of teen sexual activity and dating behavior may signal the lightning of substance abuse," said Joseph A. Califano, Jr., CASA's chairman and president and former U.S. Secretary of Health, Education and Welfare.

Other striking findings in this year's survey:

- Teens, half or more of whose friends regularly view and download Internet pornography, are more than three times likelier to smoke, drink or use illegal drugs, compared to teens who have no friends who engage in such behavior.

- Forty-four percent of high school students think that boys at their school often or sometimes "push girls to drink alcohol or take drugs in order to get the girls to have sex or do other sexual things."

"This year's survey reveals a tight connection between teen sexual behavior and substance abuse," said Califano. "This is not to say that teen sexual behavior causes substance abuse or that substance abuse causes teens to have sex, although we know that alcohol and drugs like marijuana and cocaine are sexually disinhibiting. It is to say that parents who become aware of certain dating and sexual behavior by their children should be alert to the increased likelihood of substance abuse."

Drugs and Schools

For the first time in its history, the CASA teen survey examined the frequency of physical fighting and cheating at schools where drugs are used, kept or sold. At such schools, 62 percent of students report seeing physical fights on a monthly basis, and students estimate that 54 percent of the student body regularly cheats on homework and tests, compared to 42 percent and 40 percent, respectively, at drug-free schools.

"This year's survey underscores the importance of drug-free schools and the across-the-board dysfunctionality of schools where drugs are used, kept and sold," added Califano.

Parents Are Out of Touch

Forty-four percent of parents believe that teens who abuse prescription drugs get them from their parents. Yet an overwhelming 71 percent of parents do not take any special precautions to protect prescription drugs in their homes.

Only 12 percent of parents think that a teen's number one concern is drugs, while 29 percent of teens report drugs as their biggest concern.

- Forty-five percent of teens attend parties where alcohol is available; 30 percent where marijuana is available; 10 percent where prescription drugs are available; and nine percent where cocaine or Ecstasy is available.

- Drugs have rebounded as the number one concern of teens.

- Twenty-one percent of 12 to 17 year-olds can buy marijuana in an hour or less; 40 percent can buy marijuana within a day.

- Forty-five percent of teens have friends who regularly view and download pornography from the Internet; such teens are at increased risk of smoking, drinking or using illegal drugs.

- Teens who attend religious services weekly are at less than half the risk of smoking, drinking or using illegal drugs as teens who do not attend such services.

"Parents, make sure you are aware of the dating practices of your child and get to know your child's friends," said Califano.

"Research has found that stimulant misuse is associated with alcohol or drug use disorders, criminal justice involvement, and receipt of mental health treatment."

Stimulant Use Is Linked to Depression, Drug Abuse, and Violence

Substance Abuse and Mental Health Services Administration

The Substance Abuse and Mental Health Services Administration (SAMHSA) works to reduce the negative impact of substance abuse and mental health problems on American communities by increasing the quality and availability of treatment services to persons suffering from substance abuse and mental disorders. The following viewpoint is based on the results of its 2006 National Survey on Drug Use and Health, which found that adolescents who had abused stimulants were significantly more likely to use other drugs, experience major depressive episodes, and engage in six types of violent or dangerous behavior.

"Nonmedical Stimulant Use, Other Drug Use, Delinquent Behaviors, and Depression Among Adolescents," *The NSDUH Report*, February 28, 2008, p. 4.

As you read, consider the following questions:

1. What percentage of adolescents who had abused stimulants in the past year also used marijuana? How much higher is this than the percentage of adolescents who had not tried stimulants?

2. What percentage of adolescents who had abused stimulants reported at least one type of serious delinquent behavior?

3. What percentage of adolescents who had abused stimulants also sold drugs?

In 2006, 2 percent of adolescents aged 12 to 17 (an estimated 510,000 persons) used stimulants nonmedically in the past year, a rate twice as high as that observed among adults aged 26 or older. Across adolescent age groups, the rate of past year nonmedical stimulant use in 2006 increased from 0.7 percent among youths aged 12 or 13 to 3.3 percent among those aged 16 or 17. Other research has found that stimulant misuse is associated with alcohol or drug use disorders, criminal justice involvement, and receipt of mental health treatment.

• Youths aged 12 to 17 who used stimulants nonmedically in the past year were more likely to have used other illicit drugs in the past year than youths who did not use stimulants nonmedically in the past year

• Over 71 percent of youths who used stimulants nonmedically in the past year engaged in any of six types of delinquent behavior in that period, compared with approximately 34 percent of youths who did not use stimulants nonmedically in the past year

• Almost 23 percent of youths who used stimulants nonmedically in the past year experienced a major depressive episode in the past year compared with 8.1 percent of youths who did not use stimulants nonmedically in that period

An Array of Problems Associated with Stimulant Abuse

The National Survey on Drug Use and Health (NSDUH) asks youths aged 12 to 17 questions related to their use of illicit drugs in the past year, including nonmedical use of stimulants. Nonmedical use is defined as the use of prescription-type psychotherapeutic drugs not prescribed for the respondent by a physician or used only for the experience or feeling they caused. Nonmedical use of prescription-type stimulants does not include use of over-the-counter drugs, but it does include use of methamphetamine as well as other stimulants. *Illicit drugs* refer to marijuana/hashish, cocaine (including crack), inhalants, hallucinogens, heroin, or prescription-type drugs used nonmedically.

NSDUH also asks youths aged 12 to 17 how often they engaged in the following delinquent activities during the past year: (a) getting into a serious fight at school or work, (b) taking part in a fight where a group of friends fought against another group, (c) carrying a handgun, (d) selling illegal drugs, (e) stealing or trying to steal anything worth more than $50, and (f) attacking someone with the intent to seriously hurt them.

NSDUH also includes questions for youths aged 12 to 17 to assess lifetime and past-year major depressive episode (MDE). For these estimates, MDE is defined using the diagnostic criteria set forth in the 4th edition of the *Diagnostic and Statistical Manual of Mental Disorders* (DSM-IV), which specifies a period of two weeks or longer during which there is either depressed mood or loss of interest or pleasure and at least four other symptoms that reflect a change in functioning, such as problems with sleep, eating, energy, concentration, and self-image.

This report examines past-year nonmedical use of stimulants among youths aged 12 to 17 and its association with other illicit drug use, delinquent activity, and MDE. All findings presented in this report are annual averages based on combined 2005 and 2006 NSDUH data.

Nonmedical Use of Stimulants and Other Illicit Drug Use

In 2005 and 2006, youths aged 12 to 17 who used stimulants nonmedically in the past year were more likely to have used other illicit drugs in the past year compared with youths who did not use stimulants nonmedically in the past year. For example, 70.2 percent of youths who used stimulants nonmedically in the past year also used marijuana compared with 12.1 percent of youths who did not use stimulants nonmedically in the past year.

Nonmedical Use of Stimulants and Delinquent Behavior

In 2005 and 2006, an estimated 8.7 million (34.5 percent) youths aged 12 to 17 reported that they engaged in at least one of the six queried types of delinquent behavior in the past year. Over 71 percent (approximately 360,000) of youths who used stimulants nonmedically in the past year reported any type of delinquent behavior compared with approximately 34 percent of youths who did not use stimulants nonmedically in the past year.

Youths who engaged in nonmedical stimulant use in the past year were more likely to have participated in each of the six delinquent behaviors in the past year compared with other youths. For example, almost 30 percent of youths who used stimulants nonmedically in the past year sold drugs compared with 2.8 percent of youths who did not use stimulants nonmedically in the past year.

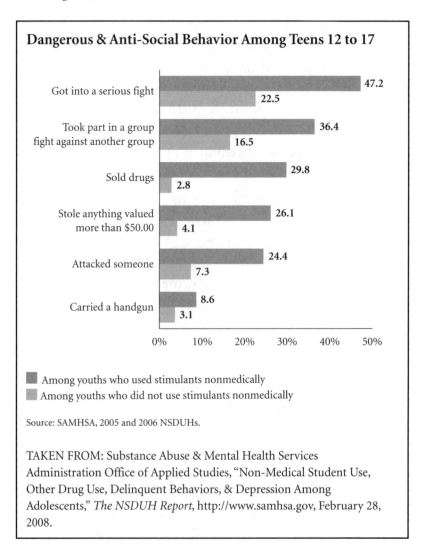

Dangerous & Anti-Social Behavior Among Teens 12 to 17

Got into a serious fight — 47.2 / 22.5

Took part in a group fight against another group — 36.4 / 16.5

Sold drugs — 29.8 / 2.8

Stole anything valued more than $50.00 — 26.1 / 4.1

Attacked someone — 24.4 / 7.3

Carried a handgun — 8.6 / 3.1

0%   10%   20%   30%   40%   50%

■ Among youths who used stimulants nonmedically
▨ Among youths who did not use stimulants nonmedically

Source: SAMHSA, 2005 and 2006 NSDUHs.

TAKEN FROM: Substance Abuse & Mental Health Services Administration Office of Applied Studies, "Non-Medical Student Use, Other Drug Use, Delinquent Behaviors, & Depression Among Adolescents," *The NSDUH Report*, http://www.samhsa.gov, February 28, 2008.

Nonmedical Use of Stimulants and Major Depressive Episode

In 2005 and 2006, an estimated 2.1 million (8.3 percent) youths aged 12 to 17 experienced at least one MDE in the past year. Youths who used stimulants nonmedically in the past year were more likely to have experienced MDE in the past year than youths who did not use stimulants nonmedically in the past year (22.8 [percent] vs. 8.1 percent).

Periodical Bibliography

The following articles have been selected to supplement the diverse views presented in this chapter.

Lori Aratani	"Teen Marijuana Use Linked to Later Illness: Self-Medication, Especially for Depression, Raises Risk of Mental Problems, Study Says," *Washington Post*, May 9, 2008.
Paul Armentano	"How to Tell If the Drug Czar Is Lying? His Lips Are Moving," LewRockwell.com, May 14, 2008.
Sarah Baldauf	"Teen Depression Worsened by Marijuana, Government Says," *U.S. News & World Report*, May 9, 2008.
Amy Harmon	"Young, Assured and Playing Pharmacist to Friends," *New York Times*, November 16, 2005.
Tim King	"New Federal Report on Marijuana Use Is Misleading, Groups Say," *Salem-News* (Salem, OR), May 10, 2008.
Medical News Today	"Teen Smoking Linked to Drinking and Drug Use," October 1, 2009. www.medicalnews today.com.
Partnership Editorial Staff	"Adderall (& Other Stimulant) Abuse on Campus," *Drug and Alcohol Scene*, May 7, 2009. http://news.drugfree.org.
Lindsey Tanner	"ADHD Drug Abuse Soars Among U.S. Teenagers," FoxNews.com, August 24, 2009.
Christian J. Teter, Sean Esteban McCabe, Kristy LaGrange, James A. Cranford, and Carol J. Boyd	"Illicit Use of Specific Prescription Stimulants Among College Students: Prevalence, Motives, and Routes of Administration," *Pharmacotherapy*, December 15, 2006.

How Can Teen Drug Abuse Be Prevented?

Chapter Preface

Nearly half of all high-school students have experimented with drugs or alcohol; some of them will ultimately drift into regular use or even dependence (or already have). It would seem to some that the community response should be similar to that used to address other public health issues, such as head lice: Screen students in order to find those that have a problem, then help them seek effective treatment. Unfortunately, implementing such a "test-and-treat" solution is not nearly as straightforward as one might hope.

Although several U.S. Supreme Court cases (most notably the 1995 case *Vernonia School District 47J v. Acton* and the 2002 case *Board of Education v. Earls*) have upheld the constitutionality of random drug testing in terms of federal law, it remains to be seen if such testing regimens are constitutional in specific states, or permissible under local law for individual school districts (suspicionless drug-testing can run afoul of state and local laws protecting the privacy of individuals, especially minors). Even if schoolwide random drug screening is found to be perfectly legal in a given school district, serious questions about the effectiveness of these programs, and even the accuracy of the drug tests themselves, remain.

Assuming that drug tests are legal and accurate, many schools and courts go on to suggest (or even mandate) rehabilitation programs or counseling. Unfortunately, while there is a dizzying variety of such programs (ranging from one-on-one and group counseling that are scheduled around school and family commitments, to long-term residential programs, and even to "boot camps," "wilderness challenges," and other intensive "tough love" programs), there is scarce research demonstrating long-term, or even short-term, effectiveness for any of these programs. By 2004, the National Institute of Health had concluded that "programs that seek to prevent [high-risk behavior] through fear and tough treatment do not work . . . and there is some evidence that they may make problems worse rather than simply not working. . . . [By] provid[ing] an opportunity for delinquent youth to amplify negative effects on each other."

The authors of the following viewpoints will present a variety of views on various tactics currently used to address adolescent drug abuse, and shed light on how these may help, or even hurt, teenagers.

1

| "I think these kinds of policies actually create more drug abuse among young people."

School Drug Testing Programs Do More Harm than Good

The Drug Reform Coordination Network

The Drug Reform Coordination Network (DRCNet) is an education, support, and advocacy organization working to end drug prohibition in favor of a "sensible framework in which drugs can be regulated and controlled." Among other positions, DRCNet argues that "suspicionless" school drug testing programs—especially random drug testing programs that include the entire school population—are questionably legal and undermine student and staff relationships. DRCNet contends the testing programs are all the more unsettling when one considers how little evidence there is that such programs prevent drug use.

As you read, consider the following questions:

1. According to the Centers for Disease Control and Prevention, how many junior high schools and high schools had random drug testing programs in 2007?

"Number of Schools Embracing Random Drug Testing on the Rise—So Is Opposition," *Drug War Chronicles*, September 26, 2008. Reproduced by permission.

2. According to the Student Drug Testing Coalition, how quickly is the number of random school drug testing programs increasing?

3. According to research by the University of Michigan's Lloyd Johnston, what impact does drug testing have on marijuana use by students as a whole, experienced marijuana users, and student athletes?

Emboldened by a pair of US Supreme Court decisions and spurred by the Bush administration's push to expand drug testing of students, an increasing number of school districts across the country are embracing drug testing as a drug abuse prevention measure. While the Office of National Drug Control Policy (ONDCP, the drug czar's office) and anti-drug activists applaud the trend, the resort to random drug testing of junior and senior high school students has also sparked a counter-movement that tries to persuade schools to instead embrace drug prevention strategies that do not treat students as guilty until proven innocent.

School Drug Testing
Is Increasingly Common

In [the cases of] *Vernonia [School District]* in 1995 and *[Lindsay] Earls* in 2002, the Supreme Court okayed the random drug testing of student athletes and students involved in extracurricular activities, respectively. Beginning in 2004, the Bush administration and drug czar John Walters began a push to get schools to create drug testing programs, seeding them with millions of dollars in federal grant money.

While earlier statistics on the number of schools resorting to student drug testing are hard to come by, the National Association of School Boards told the *Chronicle* that year [2004] that it thought the top-end figure stood at about 5%. Federal estimates at that time, put the number of schools doing random drug testing at somewhere between 500 and 2,000, or a top-end figure of about 3.5%.

"We don't take a specific position on drug testing, but we wrote briefs in support of the districts in the Supreme Court cases," said Lisa Sawyer, senior staff attorney for the National Association of School Boards. "That's because we believe in local control. We like the idea that school districts have the ability to drug test if they choose."

But by the time the Centers for Disease Control [and Prevention] published the results of its school survey in October 2007, it reported the number of schools with random drug testing programs was 4,200. That is about 7% of the nation's 59,000 junior and senior high schools.

The Student Drug Testing Coalition, an offshoot of the Drug-Free Projects Coalition, which advocates for increased random drug tests of students, put the number even higher in a May 2008 report. According to the coalition, some 14% of school districts had random drug testing policies during the 2004–2005 school year.

The Government Promotes and Funds School Drug Testing Programs

The coalition also reported that the number of school districts resorting to random drug tests is increasing by about 100 per year, or 1% annually. That number is difficult to verify, but a Google News or similar search for "student drug testing" will show that the issue is being debated by school boards across the country every week.

"When the Bush administration started pushing for testing after the *Earls* decision, schools didn't know about that policy, and the administration has had some success in convincing some districts this is a good policy to try," said Jennifer Kern, youth policy manager for the Drug Policy Alliance, which, along with groups such as Students for Sensible Drug Policy

(SSDP), the ACLU Drug Law Reform Project, and NORML [National Organization for the Reform of Marijuana Laws], is leading the charge against student drug testing. "Although they have not had much success convincing the public health and educational community this is the way to go, they have been barnstorming the country, and some districts have gone for it."

Since 2004, the drug czar's office has organized student drug testing "summits" around the country to push more districts to embrace testing and to sweeten the pot by aiding them [in applying] for federal student drug testing grants. They had been occurring at a rate of about four a year, but this year [2008] that number has jumped to eight, with two set next month for Omaha, Nebraska, and Albany, New York.

Many Students, Parents, and Teachers Oppose Drug Testing

As at past summits, the opposition will be in Omaha and Albany, said Kern. "We'll be doing what we did in the past, getting people to come out, providing materials, talking to educators, who we've found to be quite receptive to our message," she said. "Hopefully, this is the drug czar's last hurrah," she said, with an eye on the November elections.

"At past summits, most attendees were undecided about school drug testing," said SSDP executive director Kris Krane. "They wanted to hear the government's pitch and find out how to apply for grant money, but we found them generally very receptive to our points of view. We stuck to our specific concerns about drug testing, and our message was generally well received."

Opponents of student drug testing aren't limited to reform organizations. Not surprisingly, high school students themselves and their parents form another bloc where opposition can and does emerge. Kern reported being contacted by numerous students and parents as drug testing becomes an issue in their communities.

Students Make Personal Sacrifices to Protest Drug Testing

When Allentown High School in Allentown, New Jersey, instituted a drug testing program, it did so in the face of student and parent opposition, and that opposition hasn't ended. Allie Brody, a senior at Allentown High, is taking a stand against student drug testing—and it's costing her. Carrying a 3.96 Grade Point Average, Brody is a member of the National Honor Society. Last year, she was in the school travel club, founded the school philosophy club, and helped out on the school musical, among other extracurricular activities. This year, she can't do any of that because she refused to sign a consent form for drug testing.

"Drug testing goes very strongly against my principles. It is taking the choice about what happens to my body out of my parents' hands. That's not the school's responsibility, and I'm not willing to give it to them," she said. . . .

"Now I can't participate in extracurricular activities, I've been removed as vice-president of the French Honor Society, and my National Honor Society membership is in question," she said matter-of-factly. "I have to park off campus. This may even affect where I can go to college," the honor student said. "I'm making a personal statement about drug testing and I hope colleges will understand. If they don't, I don't think that's the kind of place I would want to attend anyway."

Brody and other students worked to stop the board from establishing the drug testing policy, to no avail, she said. "My friend Brendan Benedict [cofounder with Brody of Students Morally Against Drug Testing (SMART)] and I got a lot of students to come out, and my parents have been really supportive, and we've gotten a lot of support from the commu-

Not All Drug Testing Is Protected Under the Law

In 2002, by a margin of five to four, the U.S. Supreme Court in *Board of Education of Pottawatomie v. Earls* permitted public school districts to drug test students participating in competitive extracurricular activities. In its ruling, however, the Court [interpreted only] *federal* law. Schools are also subject to *state* law, which may provide greater protections for students' privacy rights. These laws vary greatly from state to state and, in many states, the law may not yet be well-defined by the courts.

Since the 2002 *Earls* decision, lawsuits have been filed in many states, including Indiana, New Jersey, Oregon, Pennsylvania, Texas and Washington, challenging school districts' drug testing policies. Most of these school districts will spend thousands of taxpayer dollars battling these lawsuits with no guarantee of success.

U.S. Supreme Court DID NOT say . . .

- The Court DID NOT say that schools are required to test students involved in competitive extracurricular activities.
- The Court DID NOT say drug testing of all students or specific groups of students outside of those participating in competitive extracurricular activities (i.e., student drivers) is constitutional.
- The Court DID NOT say it is constitutional to drug test elementary school children.
- The Court DID NOT say that it is constitutional to test by means other than urinalysis.
- The Court DID NOT say that schools are protected from lawsuits under their respective state laws.

ACLU, "Making Sense of Student Drug Testing:
Why Educators Are Saying No," www.aclu.org, January 2006.

nity. I tried to stop it by attending board meetings, but it was like the board had made up its mind before we even heard about it, and I didn't have a vote on the board."

Student Drug Testing Doesn't Reduce Drug Use

Kern and other reformers are determined to provide whatever assistance they can to students, parents, and educators opposed to student drug testing. They have prepared a kit to prepare people attending the drug czar's summits, they have created the Safety 1st web site with alternative approaches to drug testing, and even a "Drug Testing Invades My Privacy" Facebook page.

They can also point interested parties to New Mexico, where the Drug Policy Alliance has received a grant to do youth substance abuse education. The New Mexico office has just produced a new video about meth and materials for training educators.

While some of the opposition to student drug testing is moral or philosophical, opponents also cite various studies showing that drug testing has no impact on student drug use rates or even that it has a negative impact. A 2003 study headed by University of Michigan researcher Lloyd Johnston of Monitoring the Future fame put it this way:

> Drug testing still is found not to be associated with students' reported illicit drug use—even random testing that potentially subjects the entire student body. Testing was not found to have significant association with the prevalence of drug use among the entire student body nor the prevalence of use among experienced marijuana users. Analyses of male high school athletes found that drug testing of athletes in the school was not associated with any appreciably different levels of marijuana or other illicit drug use.

On the other hand, the drug czar's student drug testing web site and the Student Drug Testing Coalition's drug testing effectiveness web page offer up additional studies that attempt to rebut or refute Johnston's and similar findings.

Drug Testing Programs Damage Staff-Student Relationships

But it's not just about student drug testing's much-debated effectiveness; it's also about how schools view their students and vice versa, said SSDP's Krane.

"School drug testing really breaks down the trust between students and teachers, counselors, and administrators," he said. "If they do have a substance abuse problem, they need to see authority figures as people they can trust, not as people constantly viewing them as suspects. Drug testing tells these kids they're guilty until proven innocent," Krane continued.

"If we only drug test students in athletics and extracurricular activities, and they might be experimenting or smoking a little pot, we're actually driving them away from participating in those activities. Is that what we want?" Krane asked rhetorically. I think these kinds of policies actually create more drug abuse among young people.

Working for Change in Washington

While the battle is being fought district by district across the country, reform organizations are also keeping an eye on the prize in Washington, where Congress must decide whether to continue funding the Bush administration's drug testing grant program. While no further action is expected this year, activists are planning ahead.

School drug testing politics on Capitol Hill is done for this year [2008], [said] Krane, whose organization has fought student drug testing for years. "There is nothing to be done legislatively for the rest of the year," he said. "It looked like the ONDCP grants would be cut, the Senate version did cut it, but in the end, the Congress merged everything into an omnibus spending bill and they just re-upped at last year's spending levels."

"What we would like to see is a prohibition on using federal money to fund these student drug testing programs because funds under the Safe and Drug-Free Schools Act must go to programs that are evidence-based, and student drug testing is not evidence-based," said Kern. "But realistically, we can try to cut funding for the program and the drug czar's road trips to promote this."

Much depends on how the November [2008] election turns out, Kern said. "If we get a new drug czar who takes a public health approach to these issues, there is a really good chance of curtailing this ideologically based federal push. There is already a lot of resistance at the state and local level because random suspicionless student drug testing goes against many best practices in prevention, school environment, and relationships and trust between students and teachers."

> "The use of research-based . . . tools, re-
> view and analysis . . . provides clear
> evidence that refutes the claims of
> negative effects of [random student
> drug-testing programs] on students and
> school culture."

School Drug Testing Programs Work

C.E. Edwards

In the following viewpoint, researcher C.E. Edwards argues that random student drug-testing (RSDT) programs are effective. Citing the well-documented RSDT programs used in roughly half of the public schools in New Jersey, Edwards found that the schools were able to maintain educational environments measurably superior to their non-RSDT fellow schools, with none of the negative side effects cited by anti-RSDT advocates. This viewpoint comes from a report issued by the Student Drug Testing Coalition (a project of the Drug-Free Projects Coalition.)

C.E. Edwards, "Student Drug-testing Programs: Do These Programs Negatively Impact Students?" Drug-Free Projects Coalition, July 2008. Reproduced by permission.

As you read, consider the following questions:

1. How do daily attendance rates, graduation rates, and college admission rates compare between schools with and without random drug-testing programs?

2. What role does a "medical review officer" play in a well-run random student drug-testing program?

3. Does federal law permit schools with random drug-testing programs to inform law enforcement of positive test results?

Making the decision to add a student random drug-testing program (RSDT) to existing prevention programs should be based upon factual and accurate information, while also benefitting from the experience of more than 16 percent of U.S. secondary school districts that have implemented student drug testing programs. Factual information on student drug-testing programs is widely available, yet districts and parents considering such programs continue to be subjected to a litany of claims [without any supporting evidence] that RSDT programs negatively impact student morale and behaviors.... When closely examined, these claims are found to be conjecture or worse, opinion offered as fact and unsubstantiated by data.

Studies Refute Claims of Negative Impacts

In a review of data from the New Jersey Department of Education and individual school districts with similar demographics for the 2006–2007 school year, conducted by Christina Steffner, it was found that when comparing schools with RSDT programs to schools without programs, claims of negative impacts were unsupported. At least three additional studies have also found no evidence that RSDT programs negatively impact students.[1]

Many school districts across the U.S. have access to state report-card data similar to what is available in New Jersey. Such data can be compiled and analyzed to determine if student morale and behaviors have been negatively impacted in those districts with RSDT programs while considering the following list of frequently-cited and unsubstantiated claims of negative impacts.

Those opposing RSDT programs conjecture that such programs will:

- Decrease levels of participation in extra-curricular and after-school activities

- Create distrust between students and teachers

- Create distrust between students and administrators

- Create distrust between students and parents

1. Joseph McKinney, JD, Ed.D, "Effectiveness of random student drug-testing programs," Ball State University, August 2005. This study found that the majority of responders reported that student drug use *decreased* and that the RSDT programs did not affect student activity participation levels adversely. In fact, almost one-half of principals reported *increases in participation levels for athletic programs*. The reported per-test cost of an RSDT program was $30 or less for 91% of the 54 high schools with RSDT programs; 100% of principals responding stated that they observed no evidence of a negative impact of the prevention program upon the classroom. High schools with RSDT programs exceeded the state average for test scores on the state-mandated graduation test as well as exceeding the state average for graduation rates. Another study: Linn Goldberg, MD, FACSM et al., "Student Athlete Testing Using Random Notification Study (SATURN)," Oregon Health Sciences University, 2000-1. This study not only found no decreases in sport-activity participation by students subjected to RSDT, but that there was an 11% increase in participation following implementation of RSDT programs. Additional study: Joseph McKinney, JD, Ed.D, "It's My Call/It's Our Call (IMC/IOC) Random Student Drug Testing Program: Major Results of Year One Study," Winston-Salem/Forsyth County School System, 2006, unpublished. Preliminary results demonstrated that students in the program were far less likely to have used marijuana [or] flunked a year of school, [and] less likely to have been expelled, suspended or truant. Students in the program made better grades in school.

- Create a school atmosphere of resentment, suspicion and alienation

- Increase truancy rates

- Cause drug-use diversion to less-detectable drugs

- Breach student confidentiality if prescribed medications used

- Invade student privacy rights

- Provide a false sense of a drug-free environment

- Allow for identification of drug use without providing for a remedy

- Use school resources that should be used for education

Are these opinions supported by fact? A review of school data in New Jersey clearly demonstrates such claims of negative impacts are unsupported. In reality, the data review provides evidence to the contrary, supporting clear evidence of a positive impact at those schools with RSDT programs.

Positive, Verifiable Outcomes in New Jersey Schools

In 1975, the New Jersey Department of Education began using District Factor Groups (DFG) to classify school districts based upon socioeconomic status (SES). The DFG scale designates districts with the lowest SES as "A" and those with the highest SES as "J". The DFG scale is also used to analyze student performance on statewide assessment examinations to allow for comparisons of student performance between districts with similar characteristics. In this study, the DFG scale is used as well as enrollment data so that, where possible, schools with similar enrollment levels could be compared. The review also compared schools within the same region. All data was obtained from the 2006–2007 school report cards and appropriate district personnel. Of the 52 school districts chosen, representing 70,107 students included in this review, one-half or 26 have RSDT programs that generally include 50% to 88% of students in the testing pools and 26 do not have RSDT programs. Additionally, the 52 school districts are located throughout the state; have designated different test pools of students when there is an RSDT program; demonstrate a range of student performance; and represent all SES levels.

The overall findings in New Jersey demonstrated that daily attendance rates at schools with RSDT programs (94.8%) were higher than at non-RSDT schools (89.8%). Graduation rates were also higher at schools with RSDT (96%) than for students enrolled at non-testing schools (95.4%). Students subject to RSDT scored higher, on average, on the High School Proficiency Assessment (HSPA) and the SAT. The data also demonstrates that more students from RSDT districts go on to higher education (90.9%) as compared to their counterparts in non-testing districts (89.3%). Suspension and dropout rates were lower at schools with RSDT programs. [Whereas] there was only one (1) expulsion at an RSDT school, non-testing schools had 14 expulsions. This data clearly refutes assertions that students attending schools with RSDT programs experience a loss of connectedness with their schools as measured by indicators such as student performance on standardized tests, daily attendance, graduation, suspension, expulsion and dropout rates.

Hunterdon Central Regional High School, randomly drug testing students since 1996, has an enrollment of just under 3,200 students in grades 9–12. The statistical data from Hunterdon Central Regional High School, as well as that for the other 25 RSDT New Jersey high schools, clearly demonstrates that student participation in athletics or extra-curricular activities did not decrease. This data also serves to refute the related conjecture that risky behaviors, resulting from decreased participation, will increase.

A Comparison of New Jersey Schools With and Without Drug Testing Programs

	Random Student Drug Testing Schools	Non-testing Schools
Total number of schools	26	26
Total enrollment	37,923	39,184
Daily attendance rate	94.8%	89.8%
Graduation rate	96.0%	95.4%
Suspension rate	11.0%	15.9%
Drop-out rate	0.9%	1.1%
Expulsion rate	1	14
% of students passing state standardized tests	95.2%	91.6%
Average math, language arts, SATs	511/496	505/489
% of students going on to higher education	90.9%	89.3%

TAKEN FROM: C.E. Edwards, "Student Drug-Testing Programs: Do These Programs Negatively Impact Students?" Drug-Free Projects Coalition, July 2008.

Many Concerns Are Totally Unfounded

Student participation in activities was consistent among schools of similar demographics and locales with non-RSDT schools reporting similar levels of participation. It was found that in New Jersey districts, the level of participation was more likely to be [affected] by the DFG where it was observed that there was greater participation in school districts with a higher DFG rating.

As to creating an environment of resentment, distrust and suspicion between parent-child and/or school-child relationships leading to a loss of school connectedness and runaway behavior, the schools with RSDT programs showed no increase in runaway or truancy behaviors when compared to schools without programs.

New Jersey school districts, through the use of research-based studies such as the Rocky Mountain Behavioral Science Institute American Drug and Alcohol Survey, did not experience drug-use diversion to less detectable or non-tested drugs. Most districts construct RSDT policies that permit testing for a variety of substances and modification of the drug-test panels. Many districts also allow for a variety of specimens [samples] may be collected and tested, randomly selecting specimen type when the student reports for testing. Students, therefore, cannot be certain what drugs will be included in the test, nor do they have the opportunity to substitute specimens.

Using proven and generally accepted procedures and practices for any drug-testing program prevents breaching student confidentiality and privacy. Standard procedures include unobserved collections when the specimen is urine. Many districts contract for specimen collection with a third party. A necessary part of any correctly-structured RSDT program is the use of a Medical Review Officer (MRO). A licensed physician, the MRO is specifically trained to interpret drug-test results and reviews all positive test results. Where there is a question of legitimate use of a prescription drug, the MRO makes direct contact with a parent and obtains prescription medication information. The MRO verifies legitimate use of the substance and reports the drug-test result as 'negative' to the school representative.

U.S. public school districts with RSDT programs must adhere to specific requirements of student confidentiality as dictated by the Federal Privacy Act, the Federal Alcohol and Drug Abuse Act and federal regulation. Students are not identified by name, social security number or student identification number for drug-test purposes. All drug-testing records are maintained separate from permanent records and must be destroyed upon graduation. School district officials may not share information of a positive screen with local law enforcement agencies. Information on drug-test results may . . . be given [only] to the student and the parent. Only individuals authorized to administer the program are permitted access to drug-test results.

Drug-Testing Programs Are Part of an Integrated Response to Drug Education

All schools included in this review, as well as most others in the U.S., recognize that RSDT is only one part of a comprehensive prevention strategy that should also include drug and alcohol education programs. New Jersey public schools with RSDT programs continue to utilize multifaceted prevention strategies to meet the annual state-mandated 10 hours of drug and alcohol education for grades K-12. Campuses are not promoted as drug-free environments—but those with RSDT programs are certainly shown to be environments that maintain a clear and strong message that drug use by students is unacceptable.

New Jersey schools offer Student Assistance Programs and Student Assistance Counselors on staff as a remedy and support when there is student drug use. These professionals provide education and counseling for students who test positive. While most students do not require treatment, district policies require students who have a positive-test result to be evaluated by a licensed drug addictions counselor and to follow any recommendations made by the counselor.

Drug-Testing Does Not Divert Funds from Education

Those schools not using a third-party collector train school nurses or designated staff to administer the RSDT program. Teachers continue their work as educators and are not generally involved in RSDT programs. The cost of an RSDT program can be budgeted to meet the needs of the school district without taking time or funds from the primary role of education. School districts in New Jersey and across the U.S. have found ways to raise or re-allocate funds, obtain grant funding or other means of supporting RSDT programs. School time and resources are not diverted from the primary mission of education to administer an RSDT program.

The use of research-based and local Organizational Health Inventories (OHI) satisfaction tools, review and analysis of state report-card data used to measure performance indicators of schools and discussion with school officials in New Jersey provides clear evidence that refutes the claims of negative effects of RSDT on students and school culture. Schools with RSDT programs send a clear message about drug and alcohol use, provide students with opportunities to avoid drug and alcohol use, [and] provide a means for identification and early intervention in student drugs and alcohol use. These programs contribute to a nurturing environment that allows students to flourish and to participate in the educational process.

> "The estimated cost of DARE annually is already $1 [billion] to $1.3 billion. That's a lot for a completely ineffective, often counterproductive program."

DARE Doesn't Work

David J. Hanson, PhD.

David J. Hanson is professor emeritus of sociology at the State University of New York at Potsdam. He has researched alcohol and drinking for more than forty years, and he is a frequently cited expert on alcohol use, in addition to having written two books and numerous articles on the topic. In the following viewpoint, Hanson argues that the DARE program, although relatively inexpensive, is enormously costly because it is entirely ineffective, is possibly counterproductive, and that its supporting organization, DARE America, has proved to be antagonistic to any free and open debate of its techniques and results.

As you read, consider the following questions:

1. What change was there in drug and tobacco usage among students who participated in one DARE program in Houston, Texas?

2. What technique has repeatedly proved effective in reducing alcohol abuse among teens?

3. What three effective alternatives to DARE does the author suggest?

The Drug Abuse Resistance Education [DARE] program is used in nearly 80% of the school districts in the United States, in 54 other countries around the world, and is taught to 36,000,000 students each year. Therefore, it's important to know if this highly popular program is effective in reducing alcohol and drug use.

The Effectiveness of DARE

Scientific evaluation studies have consistently shown that DARE is ineffective in reducing the use of alcohol and drugs and is sometimes even counterproductive—worse than doing nothing. That's the conclusion of the U.S. [Government Accountability Office], the U.S. Surgeon General, the National Academy of Sciences, and the U.S. Department of Education, among many others.

The U.S. Department of Education prohibits schools from spending its funding on DARE because the program is completely ineffective in reducing alcohol and drug use.

Leaders of DARE say the program shouldn't be judged by evidence from empirical research studies. They tend to be indifferent to factual evidence and prefer to rely on feelings, impressions and hopes. As one DARE leader explained: "I don't have any statistics for you. Our strongest numbers are the numbers that don't show up."

DARE's leadership dismisses studies questioning the program's effectiveness. It's argued that the program doesn't need to be evaluated because it's based on proven educational theories and techniques.

Not so, according to the experts who should know. "World-renowned psychologists Bill Coulson, Carl Rogers, and Abraham Maslow developed the theories that DARE was founded on. Rogers and Maslow later admitted their theories were wrong and off-base. Coulson concluded that the program is 'rooted in trash psychology.'" [from Diane Barnes, "DARE Indoctrination Fails to Work & Ends Up Endangering Our Families," *Detroit News*, April 2, 2000].

If people insist on evidence, MADD [Mothers Against Drunk Driving] leadership points to surveys that ask students, parents, and teachers whether they like the program. Although irrelevant to effectiveness, most people report satisfaction with DARE. The organization's leadership argues that such satisfaction demonstrates effectiveness.

A Double-Standard for Judging Efficacy

DARE has a double standard for proof. On the one hand, it says the fact that most people like the program is proof that it's effective. On the other hand, it insists that only a nationwide study over many years and costing three to five million dollars could demonstrate that it's not effective! DARE plays a game of "heads I win, tails you lose."

When [a] National Institutes of Health/University of Kentucky study found DARE ineffective, the organization's leader [DARE founder and president, Glenn Levant] called it "bogus," an "academic fraud," and claimed that it was "part of an anti-DARE vendetta by therapists." He dismissed the results as "voodoo science" and charged, without any evidence, that DARE's critics are biased by their financial interest in prevention programs that compete with DARE. "I truly believe they are setting out to find ways to attack our programs and are misusing science to do it. The bottom line is that they don't want police officers to do the work, because they want it for themselves."

Proponents seem inclined to ignore scientific research findings. [According to Tana Dineen, "'Just Say No' to Feel-Good, Time-Wasters Like DARE," *Alberta Report*, Feb 19, 2001]

"I'll trade you a peanut butter sandwich for your meds," cartoon by Joe di Chiarro. www.CartoonStock.com

"In Houston, Texas, where a study showed a shocking 29% increase in drug usage and a 34% increase in tobacco usage among students participating in DARE, the police chief defended it by saying he would use the results to 'fine-tune the program to better serve the children.'" And he unashamedly promoted spending $3.7 million on DARE in the city.

DARE leaders not only tend to ignore scientific evidence but even challenge science itself. On one occasion, when confronted with the scientific evidence found by a major study, DARE leadership retorted that "Scientists tell you that bumblebees can't fly, but we know better." Of course, scientists don't tell us that bumblebees can't fly, and this statement illustrates a complete lack of any understanding of science. Similarly, the leadership sometimes seems to dismiss scientific evidence as nothing more than opinion or preference.

DARE Attacks or Ignores Critics

"Our detractors like to characterize DARE as an 'Orwellian [resembling the totalitarian world portrayed in George Orwell's novel *Nineteen-Eighty-Four*] reality' or 'Big Brother' at work," says DARE. "These bush-league tactics are transparent for what they are: attempts to support various individual personal agendas at the expense of our children."

A DARE press release titled "Pro-Drug Groups Behind Attack on Prevention Programs" damns any who criticize DARE as being advocates of drug legalization. DARE leadership has questioned the motives of anyone who doubts the program in any way. Sometimes DARE suggests that critics are just jealous of the organization's success. The DARE position is that the program works fine; the only problem is with evaluators and anyone who criticizes it.

This is unfortunate and counterproductive. As a DARE supporter points out "The group is its own worst enemy because it has spent so much effort attacking the evaluators, rather than learning from research."

DARE Stifles Discussion of the Program's Effectiveness

[According to Jodi Upton, "DARE Wary of Outside Reviews," *Detroit News*, February 27, 2000] "In 1986, a National Institute of Justice study suggested that DARE had some promise. The timing was perfect. First Lady Nancy Reagan was admonishing kids to 'Just Say No.' And Congress soon approved a large package of drug prevention money, earmarking 10 percent to go to programs taught by uniformed cops. Along with other criteria, the set-aside perfectly matched DARE, launching the program nationally."

Does DARE Cause Substance Abuse?

A number of controlled studies of substance-abuse-prevention programs, particularly those targeted at preventing drug use, have shown iatrogenic effects [illness caused by medical examination or treatment]. The best known and most popular of these programs is DARE, which uses uniformed police officers to teach schoolchildren (a) about the risks of drug use and (b) social skills to resist peer pressure to try drugs. Most research indicates that DARE is largely or entirely ineffective. . . . Moreover, the results of several RCTs [randomized controlled trials] and quasi-experimental studies suggest that DARE and similar programs based on resisting social influence may actually increase intake of alcohol and perhaps other drugs. . . .

Moreover, some PHTs [potentially harmful treatments] may appear to be efficacious because many individuals overestimate the prevalence of negative effects without treatment. . . . Many parents and proponents of DARE programs may similarly conclude that these interventions are efficacious because they overestimate the number of children and adolescents who engage in drug abuse. Consequently, advocates of DARE may accurately observe that some children and adolescents engage in problematic behaviors following this intervention but fail to attribute these behaviors to the negative effects of treatment. . . .

The probable negative effects of some DARE programs on substance abuse intake may be attributable to the inadvertent normalization of the use of relatively mild substances (e.g., alcohol) resulting from an excessive focus on severe substances (e.g., cocaine, heroin).

Scott O. Lilienfeld,
"Psychological Treatments That Cause Harm,"
Perspectives on Psychological Science, *April 27, 2007.*

However, a peer review of the study soon identified major problems. In reality, the results suggested that DARE might actually increase drug use among girls. The U.S. Bureau of Justice Assistance then funded a follow-up study by the Research Triangle Institute (RTI), a nationally prestigious research organization that had never had a study go unpublished. Before the study was completed, RTI "started finding that DARE simply didn't work," and released preliminary findings at a conference.

"The national DARE organization kicked into high gear: such information could never been seen by the public. The group made threatening phone calls and violent threats to researchers, determined to hide the information." [According to Adam Hunter, *Hermes Magazine*] RTI didn't publish its study.

When it became known that the prestigious *American Journal of Public Health* planned to publish the study, DARE strongly objected and tried to prevent publication. "DARE has tried to interfere with the publication of this. They tried to intimidate us," the publication director reported.

After his story questioning the effectiveness of DARE appeared in *USA Today*, reporter Dennis Cauchon "received letters from classrooms in different parts of the country, all addressed to 'Dear DARE-basher,' and all using near-identical language." He says that DARE also tried to intimidate *USA Today* with a lawsuit.

When NBC planned a news magazine feature on the program, DARE cooperated until it became apparent that the story wasn't going to be simply a puff-piece. "They worked very hard to get our story suppressed," the producer says. After interviewing a critic of DARE, the producer was angrily confronted by a national DARE official, who demanded to know why they were "talking to a pro-marijuana supporter."

In a case involving DARE's libel suit against *Rolling Stone* magazine for a critical article, a federal judge ruled that there was "substantial truth" to the charges in the article, that DARE had sought to "suppress scientific research" critical of DARE and had "attempted to silence researchers at the Research Triangle Institute, editors at the *American Journal of Public Health*, and producers at *Dateline: NBC.*"

Effective Alternatives to DARE

The social norms marketing technique has repeatedly proven effective in reducing the use and abuse of alcohol among young people. It's based on the fact that the vast majority of young people greatly exaggerate in their minds the quantity and frequency of drinking among their peers. Therefore, they tend to drink—or drink more—than they would otherwise, in an effort to "fit in."

When credible surveys demonstrate the actual, much lower drinking rates, and the results are widely publicized or "marketed" to this group, the imagined social pressure drops and so does youthful drinking. The technique works with both alcohol and drugs.

And if this weren't enough, the technique costs very little to implement. . . .

Brief intervention techniques have also proven effective. . . .

In addition, the U.S. Department of Education has identified the following programs as effective for specific target groups. They include:

- *Life Skills Training Program* (LST)—LST is a school-based substance abuse prevention program for students 10–14 years of age. It teaches general personal and social skills, specific resistance skills, and normative information.

- *Project ALERT*—Project ALERT is also a school-based program, in this case for students in middle school. It teaches drug abstention norms, reasons to abstain, and resistance skills.

- *Strengthening Families Program* (SFP)—SFP is a substance abuse prevention program for substance-abusing families with children six to twelve years of age.

While they are limited to restricted target groups, the major disadvantage of these three programs is their cost, which is high to very high. But because they are effective, they are bargains compared to the completely ineffective DARE program.

With all of the effective programs available, there is simply no excuse to continue using the useless and sometimes counterproductive DARE program. It's important to remember that DARE is expensive in terms of both money and time. Every hour devoted to DARE is an hour lost to math, reading, or even to an effective abuse prevention program.

Our young people deserve much better.

Important Facts About DARE

- DARE has been charged with "cribbing" its program from a curriculum developed by someone else without that researcher's permission.

- One researcher discovered that DARE was misrepresenting his findings on its web site to imply that he had found it effective in the long term, which he had not.

- "It's well established that DARE doesn't work." Dr. Gilbert Botvin, Cornell Medical Center.

- "Research shows that, no, DARE hasn't been effective in reducing drug use." William Modzeleski, top drug education official at the Department of Education.

- "I think the program should be entirely scrapped and redeveloped anew." Dr. William Hansen, who helped design the original DARE curriculum.

- DARE is "a fraud on the people of America," says the mayor of Salt Lake City, asserting that "For far too long our drug-prevention policies have been driven by mindless adherence to a wasteful, ineffective, feel-good program."

Changes and "Improvements" to DARE Work No Better

"Anything is better than nothing, but common sense says more is better," DARE leadership says. DARE's solution is to expand DARE by beginning it in earlier grades and extending it to higher grades. More of an ineffective program can't make it effective. Apparently the head of DARE also thinks a dog could catch its tail if only it could run faster.

DARE has made about a dozen revisions to its program. Each time another study reports that the program is ineffective, DARE responds by saying that the results apply to "the old program." Each revision has proven to be just as ineffective as the one it follows, but it's a very effective tactic to distract and confuse the public.

DARE is testing another revision. However, it remains essentially the same, "with only superficial changes. The same student handbook will be used, with the same messages that do not work." [according to the Michigan State University School of Criminal Justice] Preliminary evaluations have found the rates of alcohol and drug use among students participating in the "new" DARE program to be the same as those among students using the old, failed DARE.

[According to Dawn MacKeen, "Just Say No to DARE," Salon.com, February 16, 2001] "Critics of DARE say the time is long overdue to dismantle the program and make sure, before exposing children to it, that it is not only effective but, most important, not harmful. They also worry that these changes, like much-heralded changes in the past, will not be significant enough to completely revamp the failing program."

The Likelihood of Doing Harm

"It's a mistake to assume that you can simply design a program and know in advance whether it will be harmful," says Dr. Joan McCord, a leading expert on evaluating programs. "I think of those who created thalidomide [a drug that was found to cause severe birth defects]. They had good intentions, and look what happened. The harm comes from the failure of programs, and programs must be evaluated for safety."

DARE argues that "if D.A.R.E. detoured just one child. . . ." communities should support it. Yet if a drug worked one percent of the time, the Food and Drug Administration would pull it off the market. Many experts assert that politics is what has kept the much-criticized program around for so many years, despite a mountain of evidence that it's not only ineffective but sometimes even counterproductive and causing harm to young people.

The estimated cost of DARE annually is already $1 [billion] to 1.3 billion. That's a lot for a completely ineffective, often counterproductive program.

> *"Tough love programs are ineffective, based on pseudoscience, and rooted in a brutal ideology that produces more harm than most of the problems they are supposedly aimed at addressing."*

"Tough Love" Drug Treatment Doesn't Work

Maia Szalavitz

Maia Szalavitz is a journalist best known for reporting on science, health, and public policy; she often writes about developments in the multibillion dollar teen "tough love" rehabilitation industry. In the following viewpoint, the author presents abuse stories from "tough love" rehabilitation camps for drug abusers and troubled teens. Szalavitz notes that such programs have been proved ineffective and produce further harm.

As you read, consider the following questions:

1. According to the article, how many teenagers are currently held in "tough love" treatment programs?

2. What is one example of some of the extreme "attack therapy" methods used in The Seed rehab program?

3. According to Szalavitz, do the media present positive or negative anecdotes of "tough love" camps?

The state of Florida tortured 14-year-old Martin Lee Anderson to death for trespassing. The teen had been sentenced to probation in 2005 for taking a joy ride in a Jeep Cherokee that his cousins stole from his grandmother. Later that year, he crossed the grounds of a school on his way to visit a friend, a violation of his probation. His parents were given a choice between sending him to boot camp and sending him to juvenile detention. They chose boot camp, believing, as many Americans do, that "tough love" was more likely to rehabilitate him than prison.

Less than three hours after his admission to Florida's Bay County Sheriff's Boot Camp on January 5, 2006, Anderson was no longer breathing. He was taken to a hospital, where he was declared dead early the next morning.

A video recorded by the camp shows up to 10 of the sheriff's "drill instructors" punching, kicking, slamming to the ground, and dragging the limp body of the unresisting adolescent. Anderson had reported difficulty breathing while running the last of 16 required laps on a track, a complaint that was interpreted as defiance. When he stopped breathing entirely, this too was seen as a ruse.

Ammonia was shoved in the boy's face; this tactic apparently had been used previously to shock other boys perceived as resistant into returning to exercises. The guards also applied what they called "pressure points" to Anderson's head with their hands, one of many "pain compliance" methods they had been instructed to impose on children who didn't immediately do as they were told.

All the while, a nurse in a white uniform stood by, looking bored. At one point she examined the boy with a stethoscope, then allowed the beating to continue until he was unconscious. An autopsy report issued in May [2006]—after an initial, disputed report erroneously attributed Anderson's death to a blood disorder—concluded that he had died of suffocation, due to the combined effects of ammonia and the guards' covering his mouth and nose.

Every time a child dies in a tough love program, politicians say—as Florida Gov. Jeb Bush initially did on hearing of Anderson's death—that it is "one tragic incident" that should not be used to justify shutting such programs down. But there have now been nearly three dozen such deaths and thousands of reports of severe abuse in programs that use corporal punishment, brutal emotional attacks, isolation, and physical restraint in an attempt to reform troubled teenagers.

Tough love has become a billion-dollar industry. Several hundred programs, both public and private, use the approach. Somewhere between 10,000 and 100,000 teenagers are currently held in treatment programs based on the belief that adolescents must be broken (mentally, and often physically as well) before they can be fixed. Exact numbers are impossible to determine, because no one keeps track of the kids in these programs, most of which are privately run. The typical way to end up in a government-run program, such as the camp where Martin Lee Anderson was killed, is for a court to give you the option of going there instead of prison. The typical way to end up in a private program is to be sent there by your parents, though judges and public schools have been known to send kids to private boot camps as well. Since they offer "treatment," some of the private centers are covered by health insurance.

In the nearly five decades since the first tough love residential treatment community, Synanon, introduced the idea of attack therapy as a cure for drug abuse, hundreds of thousands of young people have undergone such "therapy." These programs have both driven and been driven by the war on drugs. Synanon, for example, was aimed at fighting heroin addiction [with] draconian methods justified by appeals to parents' fears that drugs could do far worse things to their children than a little rough treatment could. The idea was that only a painful experience of "hitting bottom" could end an attachment to the pleasures of drugs.

But like the drug war itself, tough love programs are ineffective, based on pseudoscience, and rooted in a brutal ideology that produces more harm than most of the problems they are supposedly aimed at addressing. The history of tough love shows how fear consistently trumps data [to sell] parents and politicians on a product that hurts kids.

Attack Therapy

Synanon was a supposedly utopian California community founded in 1958 by an ex-alcoholic named Chuck Dederich. Dederich believed he could improve on the voluntary 12-step program of Alcoholics Anonymous. Rather than rely on people choosing to change, Synanon would use extreme peer pressure and even physical coercion to impose the confession, surrender, and service to others that 12-step programs suggest as the road to recovery.

At the time, heroin addiction was seen as incurable. But when a heroin addict kicked drugs after participating in Dederich's brutally confrontational encounter groups, the founder and other members began living communally and promoting Synanon as an addiction cure.

The media took note, and soon state officials from across the country were visiting and setting up copycat programs back home to treat addicts. Only New Jersey bothered to do an outcome study before replicating Synanon. The investigation, released in 1969, found that only 10 to 15 percent of participants stayed in the program for more than a few months and actually ended their addictions, a rate no better than that achieved without treatment. A 1973 study of encounter groups by the Stanford psychiatrist Irvin Yalom and his colleague Morton Lieberman found that 9 percent of participants experienced lasting psychological damage and that Synanon groups were among those with the highest numbers of casualties.

But the research didn't matter. To both the media and the politicians, anecdote was evidence. The idea that toughness was the answer had a deep appeal to those who saw drug use as sin and punishment as the way to redemption. And Synanon produced testimonials worthy of a revival meeting. Indeed, it eventually recast itself as the "Church of Synanon."

By the early 1970s, the federal government itself had funded its own Synanon clone. It was located in Florida and known as The Seed.

In this program, teenagers who were using drugs or who were believed to be at risk of doing so would spend 10-to-12-hour days seated on hard-backed chairs and waving furiously to catch the attention of staffers, most of whom were former participants themselves. Like Arnold Horshack in [the TV series] *Welcome Back, Kotter* but with more desperate urgency, they would flutter their hands, begging to be called on to confess their bad behavior. Even before the excesses of the '80s, parents were so frightened of drugs that they were willing to surrender their children to strangers for tough treatment to avoid even the possibility of addiction; some parents even hit their children themselves at Seed meetings, following the instructions of program leaders.

In 1974 Sen. Sam Ervin, the North Carolina Democrat best known for heading the congressional committee that investigated Watergate, presented a report to Congress entitled "Individual Rights and the Federal Role in Behavior Modification." Ervin and other members of Congress were concerned about federal funding for efforts to change people's behavior against their will, seeing a fundamental threat to liberty if such efforts were successful. The report cited The Seed as an example of programs that "begin by subjecting the individual to isolation and humiliation in a conscious effort to break down his psychological defenses." It concluded that such pro-

Drug Treatment Can Encourage Drug Abuse

A 1998 study of nearly 150 teenagers treated in dozens of centers across the country found that there was 202 percent more crack abuse *following* treatment and a 13 percent increase in alcohol abuse. In other words, recent research suggests that parents and schools may be sending binge-drinking/social marijuana smokers off to treatment and getting back crackheads in their stead.

Maia Szalavitz, "Trick or Treatment,"
Slate.com, January 3, 2003.

grams are "similar to the highly refined brainwashing techniques employed by the North Koreans in the early 1950s."

Straight Incorporated

Ervin's report led Congress to cut off The Seed's funding. But The Seed had produced two important true believers: Mel Sembler, who went on to serve as campaign finance chairman for the Republican Party during the 2000 election season and as U.S. ambassador to Italy from 2001 to 2005, and Joseph Zappala, who would go on to serve under the first President Bush as ambassador to Spain and who at the time was also a major Republican campaign donor.

In 1976 Sembler and Zappala founded a program virtually identical to The Seed, staffed by former Seed parents and participants (including some who had become Seed staffers). They named it Straight Incorporated. The federal agency that had funded The Seed, the Law Enforcement Assistance Agency, had been barred from funding further human experiments because neither the agency nor projects like The Seed had procedures for informed consent. Despite that fact, and despite the congressional critique of The Seed, Straight soon received federal money from the same agency. It, too, never informed parents that it was experimental.

Straight expanded rapidly in the '80s, around the same time newspapers, TV, and other media were filled with dire warnings about the dangers of crack. Nancy Reagan called it her "favorite" drug program. In fact, it was a visit to Straight, suggested by Sembler, that had inspired the first lady to make drugs her cause.

An undated issue of Straight's newsletter, Epidemic, from around this time carried a photo of the legs of a young-looking corpse with a tag on one toe: "Cocaine, crack and kids." The accompanying article said crack was "almost instantaneously addictive"—"the most addictive drug known to man"—and passed along the tale of a 16-year-old girl who had recently tried smoking cocaine. "One night I noticed a big lump on my back," she wrote. "I was rushed to the hospital and operated on and had two tumors removed. The tumors were caused by impurities in the coke which built up in my blood and got infected." Such a story, if true, would have made medical history.

But for the media, drugs act as an anti-skeptic; the scarier the consequences, the bigger the story, the higher the ratings, and the lower the incentive to qualify extreme claims. The 1986 documentary *48 Hours on Crack Street* purported to show the crack menace spreading ineluctably to the middle class. It drew one of the largest TV audiences ever for a news program. . . .

"Boot Camps"

Richard Bradbury, whose activism eventually helped shut Straight down, was forcibly enrolled in the program in 1983, when he was 17. His sister had had a drug problem, and Straight demanded that he be screened for one as well. After an eight-hour interrogation in a tiny room, Bradbury, who was not an addict, was nonetheless held. He later described beatings and continuous verbal assaults, which for him centered on sexual abuse he'd suffered as a young boy. Staffers and other participants called him a "faggot," told him he'd led his abusers on, and forced him to admit "his part" in the abuse.

Straight ultimately paid out millions of dollars in dozens of lawsuits related to abuse and even kidnapping and false imprisonment of adults. But the Straight network remained in operation until 1993. . . .

Meanwhile, other organizations found they could profit from tough love with legal impunity. As negative publicity finally began to hurt Straight and skepticism about the drug war itself grew, other groups began to use similar tactics, all converging on a combination of rigid rules, total isolation of participants from both family and the outside world, constant emotional attacks, and physical punishments. These programs were sold as responses not just to drug use but to teenage "defiance," "disobedience," "inattention," and other real or imagined misbehavior.

Military-style "boot camps" came into vogue in the early '90s as an alternative to juvenile prison. The media spread fears of a new generation of violent, teenaged "super-predators," and this solution gained political appeal across the spectrum. Liberals liked that it wasn't prison and usually meant a shorter sentence than conventional detention; conservatives liked the lower costs, military style, and tough discipline. Soon "hoods in the woods" programs, which took kids into the wilderness and used the harsh environment, isolation, and spare rations to similar ends, also rose in popularity, as did "emotional growth" schools, which used isolation and Synanon-style confrontational groups.

Again, little evidence ever supported these programs. When the U.S. Department of Justice began studying the boot camps, it found that they were no more effective than juvenile prison.

For a 1997 report to Congress, the department funded a review of the research, which found that the boot camps were ineffective and that there was little empirical support for wilderness programs. In late 2004 the National Institutes of Health released a state-of-the-science consensus statement on dealing with juvenile violence and delinquency. It said that programs that seek to change behavior through "fear and tough treatment appear ineffective."

Growth of Tough Love

But as the Martin Lee Anderson case makes clear, tough love continued to thrive. Indeed, the *New York Times* business section reported on tough teen programs as an investment opportunity last year [2006], saying the number of teenagers attending residential programs to deal with drug and behavior problems had quadrupled since 1995. Exposés of programs like Straight or Florida's government-run boot camps almost always include positive anecdotes along with the accounts of abuse. As a result, for parents terrified of drugs, these stories seem to portray the programs as the only ones tough enough to "do what works." Since the media play positive anecdote against negative anecdote, often without citing the negative research data, exposés can actually serve as advertisements. The suggestion that the programs work serves to justify any abuse. In 2004, for example, *Time* quoted a father who said a tough-love program "improved his [son's] attitude and sense of responsibility," even as it reported that the family removed the child after finding some of the program's disciplinary measures too harsh. . . .

In both public and private programs, policies on the use of force are far less stringent than they are for adult prisoners or psychiatric patients. At the government-run boot camp where Anderson died, for example, restraint, punches, and kicks were routinely applied to teens to punish them for not completing exercise, for "whimpering," or for "breathing heavily." ... In a prison or mental hospital, by contrast, force is officially permitted only if the prisoner or patient is an immediate threat to himself or others. Parents who engaged in such practices could be charged with child abuse.

And the parents who send their kids to these camps? For the most part, they are uninformed about the absence of evidence supporting tough love programs and often desperate to save their kids from drugs and delinquency. Until we figure out a better balance between the right of parents to place their kids in whatever programs they choose and the right of kids to be free from inappropriate punishment by agents of their parents or the state, the abuse will continue. The shame of it all is that we know hurting kids doesn't help them.

> *"When practiced faithfully, evidence-based therapies give users their best chance to break a habit."*

Evidence-Based Drug Treatment Does Work

Benedict Carey

Benedict Carey has written on science and medicine for the New York Times *since 2004, and he has written on health for more than a decade. In the following viewpoint, the author discusses the cluttered field of rehabilitation programs—which has no standardized set of guidelines, and very infrequently tracks long-term outcomes or attempts to verify the effectiveness of its methods. Increasingly, states are mandating that publicly funded programs rely on "evidence-based" techniques; that is, those techniques which are the result of recognized scientific research and have established track records for positive, lasting results.*

As you read, consider the following questions:

1. What is the "motivational interview" technique?

2. What is "practice-based evidence"?

3. What improvements did Delaware's rehabilitation system see between 2001 and 2006, after adopting evidence-based practices and benchmarks?

Their first love might be the rum or vodka or gin and juice that is going around the bonfire. Or maybe the smoke, the potent marijuana that grows in the misted hills here [Roseburg, Oregon] like moss on a wet stone.

But it hardly matters. Here as elsewhere in the country, some users start early, fall fast and in their reckless prime can swallow, snort, inject or smoke anything available, from crystal meth to prescription pills to heroin and ecstasy. And treatment, if they get it at all, can seem like a joke.

A Revolving Door for a Chronic Problem

"After the first couple of times I went through, they basically told me that there was nothing they could do," said Angella, a 17-year-old from the central Oregon city of Bend, who by freshman year in high school was drinking hard liquor every day, smoking pot and sampling a variety of harder drugs. "They were like, 'Uh, I don't think so.'"

She tried residential programs twice, living away from home for three months each time. In those, she learned how dangerous her habit was, how much pain it was causing others in her life. She worked on strengthening her relationship with her grandparents, with whom she lived. For two months or so afterward she stayed clean.

"Then I went right back," Angella said in an interview. "After a while, you know, you just start missing your friends."

Every year, state and federal governments spend more than $15 billion, and insurers at least $5 billion more, on substance-abuse treatment services for some four million people. That amount may soon increase sharply: last year [2007], Congress passed the mental health parity law, which for the first time includes addiction treatment under a federal law requiring that insurers cover mental and physical ailments at equal levels.

Many clinics across the county have waiting lists, and researchers estimate that some 20 million Americans who could benefit from treatment do not get it.

High Demand, but Little Evidence Programs Work

Yet very few rehabilitation programs have the evidence to show that they are effective. The resort-and-spa private clinics generally do not allow outside researchers to verify their published success rates. The publicly supported programs spend their scarce resources on patient care, not costly studies.

And the field has no standard guidelines. Each program has its own philosophy; so, for that matter, do individual counselors. No one knows which approach is best for which patient, because these programs rarely if ever track clients closely after they graduate. Even Alcoholics Anonymous, the best known of all the substance-abuse programs, does not publish data on its participants' success rate.

"What we have in this country is a washing-machine model of addiction treatment," said A. Thomas McClellan, chief executive of the nonprofit Treatment Research Institute, based in Philadelphia. "You go to Shady Acres for 30 days, or to some clinic for 60 visits or 60 doses, whatever it is. And then you're discharged and everyone's crying and hugging and feeling proud—and you're supposed to be cured."

He added: "It doesn't really matter if you're a movie star going to some resort by the sea or a homeless person. The system doesn't work well for what for many people is a chronic, recurring problem."

In recent years state governments, which cover most of the bill for addiction services, have become increasingly concerned, and some, including Delaware, North Carolina and

Oregon, have sought ways to make the programs more accountable. The experience of Oregon, which has taken the most direct and aggressive action, illustrates both the promise and perils of trying to inject science into addiction treatment.

Evidence-Based Treatments

In 2003 the Oregon Legislature mandated that rehabilitation programs receiving state funds use evidence-based practices—techniques that have proved effective in studies. The law, phased in over several years, was aimed at improving services so that addicts like Angella would not be doomed to a lifetime of rehab, repeating the same kinds of counseling that had failed them in the past—or landing in worse trouble.

"You can get through a lot of programs just by faking it," said Jennifer Hatton, 25, of Myrtle Creek, Ore., a longtime drinker and drug user who quit two years ago, but only after going to jail and facing the prospect of losing her children. "That's what did it for me—my kids—and I wish it didn't have to come to that."

When practiced faithfully, evidence-based therapies give users their best chance to break a habit. Among the therapies are prescription drugs [like naltrexone for alcohol dependence, and buprenorphine for narcotics addiction], which studies find can help people kick their habits.

Another is called the motivational interview, a method intended to harden clients' commitment upon entering treatment. In M.I., as it is known, the counselor, through skilled questioning, has the addict explain why he or she has a problem, and why it is important to quit and set goals. Studies find that when clients mark their path in this way—instead of hearing the lecture from a counselor, as in many traditional programs—they stay in treatment longer.

Psychotherapy techniques in which people learn to expect and tolerate restless or low moods are also on the list. So is cognitive behavior therapy, in which addicts learn to question assumptions that reinforce their habits (like "I'll never make friends who don't do drugs") and to engage their nondrug activities and creative interests.

Evidence-Based Treatments in Action

For Angella, this kind of counseling made a difference. She spent several months in a program run by Adapt, an addiction treatment center here in Roseburg, a small city about 175 miles south of Portland.

In treatment, she said, she learned how to "just be with, and feel" bad moods without turning to drink or drugs; and to throw herself into creative projects like collage and painting. The program has helped her reconnect with her father and to enroll in college beginning in January.

"I want to be a teacher, and someone at the program is advising me on that," she said in an interview. "That's the plan, to just move out and away from my old life."

A friend of hers in the program, Alex, a 16-year-old from Roseburg, said that the therapy helped him monitor his own emotional ups and downs, without being swept away by them. The counselors "are always asking about our stress level, our anger, so you become more aware and have a better idea what to do with it," he said.

The Gap Between What They Want to Do and What They Can Afford

Almost 54 percent of Oregon's $94 million budget for addiction treatment services now goes to programs that deploy evidence-based techniques, according to a state report completed last month [November 2008]. The estimated rate before the mandate was 25 to 30 percent. The state has not yet analyzed the impact of this change on clients.

"Before the mandate, most programs had some evidence-based practices, and since then there has been a lot more interest and awareness of them," said Traci Rieckmann, a public

Addressing the Unique Needs of Teen Substance Abusers

Adolescent drug abusers have unique needs stemming from their immature neurocognitive and psychosocial stage of development. Research has demonstrated that the brain undergoes a prolonged process of development and refinement, from birth to early adulthood, during which a developmental shift occurs where actions go from more impulsive to more reasoned and reflective. In fact, the brain areas most closely associated with aspects of behavior such as decision making, judgment, planning, and self-control undergo a period of rapid development during adolescence.

Adolescent drug abuse is also often associated with other co-occurring mental health problems. These include attention-deficit hyperactivity disorder (ADHD), oppositional defiant disorder, and conduct problems, as well as depressive and anxiety disorders. This developmental period has also been associated with physical and/or sexual abuse and academic difficulties.

Adolescents are also especially sensitive to social cues, with peer groups and families being highly influential during this time. Therefore, treatments that facilitate positive parental involvement, integrate other systems in which the adolescent participates (such as school and athletics), and recognize the importance of prosocial peer relationships are among the most effective. Access to comprehensive assessment, treatment, case management, and family-support services that are developmentally, culturally, and gender-appropriate is also integral when addressing adolescent addiction.

Medications for substance abuse among adolescents may also be helpful. Currently, the only Food and Drug Administration (FDA)-approved addiction medication for adolescents is the transdermal nicotine patch.

National Institute on Drug Abuse, Principles of Drug Addiction Treatment: A Research Based Guide *(2nd Edition), April 2009.*

health researcher at Oregon Health and Science University, who is following the policy implementation with support from the Robert Wood Johnson Foundation and the National Institutes of Health.

Yet interest and awareness may not translate into good practice, and Dr. Rieckmann says it is not at all clear how many rehabilitation programs claiming to use evidence-based techniques actually do so faithfully. About 400 programs receive state money, and most of them are small, rural outfits that are already stretched to provide counseling, to say nothing of paying for extensive training.

"You're talking about therapies, like cognitive behavior therapy, that take time to learn," said John Gardin, the behavioral health and research director at Adapt in Roseburg, who travels the country to teach the skills. "Most places don't have a person like me to do that training, so they're getting two to three days of training, if that; and that's just not enough time to get it."

In studies looking at hundreds of programs nationwide, researchers have found a similar gap between what programs may want to do and what they're able to do. "For instance, most programs don't have an M.D. on staff," said Aaron Johnson, a sociologist at the University of Georgia who has led many of the studies. "Without that, of course, you can't prescribe any medications."

Tim Hartnett, the executive director of a Portland treatment program called CODA Inc., which does its own research on patient outcomes, said that the mandate had raised the level of conversation statewide, but that true reform would mean "an integrated system that tracks clients as they move from residential to outpatient treatment, and that defines clear targets" for what a person should expect from each kind of program.

"Our goal at CODA is to create a system of care that uses evidence-based practices at just the right dose and just the right time," Mr. Hartnett said. "As with many chronic diseases figuring out dosage and timing are critical."

Resistance to Change

For some addicts, a standard program may not help at all, according to Anne Fletcher, who for her book *Sober for Good* interviewed 222 men and women who had been clean for at least five years. "A lot of these people overcame an alcohol problem on their own, or with the help of an individual therapist," Ms. Fletcher said.

To complicate matters in Oregon, the state mandate has stirred a kind of culture clash between those who want reform—academic researchers, state officials—and veteran counselors working in the trenches, many of whom have beaten addictions of their own and do not appreciate outsiders telling them how to do their jobs.

"I'm a counselor, and I'd be defensive, too: 'What do you mean, all this stuff I've been doing my entire life is wrong?'" said Brian Serna, director of outpatient services at Adapt, who has traveled the state to monitor the use of scientific practices. "So the challenge is to build a bridge between what the science says is effective and what people are already doing."

Evidence-Based Practice and "Practice-Based Evidence"

One way to do that, some experts now believe, is to combine evidence-based practice with "practice-based evidence"—the results that programs and counselors themselves can document, based on their own work. In 2001 the Delaware Division of Substance Abuse and Mental Health began giving treatment programs incentives, or bonuses, if they met certain benchmarks. The clinics could earn a bonus of up to 5 percent, for instance, if they kept a high percentage of addicts coming in at least weekly and ensured that those clients met their own goals, as measured both by clean urine tests and how well they functioned in everyday life, in school, at work, at home.

By 2006, the state's rehabilitation programs were operating at 95 percent capacity, up from 50 percent in 2001; and 70 percent of patients were attending regular treatment sessions, up from 53 percent, according to an analysis of the policy published last summer in the journal Health Policy.

"We basically gave them a list of evidence-based practices and told them to pick the ones they wanted to use," said Jack Kemp, former director of substance abuse services for Delaware, in an interview. "It was up to them to decide what to use."

For those who are trying not to use [drugs or alcohol], it doesn't much matter how rehab services are improved—only that it happens in time. "Honestly, you just don't care how or why something works for you," said Ms. Hatton, the 25-year-old from Myrtle Creek, Ore. "Just that it does."

| *"The Meth Project works because of the strategic manner in which it was shaped and the frequent testing of its efforts."*

Intelligently Run Anti-Drug Ad Campaigns Do Work

William Mercer

William Mercer has served as the United States Attorney for the District of Montana since 2001. During this period Montana saw a spike in methamphetamine abuse, especially among teens. This prompted the formation of the Montana Meth Project, which was ranked as the fifth most effective nonprofit foundation in the world in 2009. The Montana Meth Project ad campaign has been highly controversial, with many characterizing its thirty-second television spots as tiny, startling horror films. According to Mercer, this controversial and confrontational approach has been vital to the campaign, which he credits with Montana's steep reduction in teen meth use.

As you read, consider the following questions:

1. What three qualities of the Montana Meth Project have made it more effective than other anti-drug advertising campaigns?

William Mercer, "Meth Project Proves Effective," *Independent Record (Helena, MT)*, December 13, 2009. Copyright © 2009, helenair.com. Reproduced by permission.

2. What percentages of Montana teens reported using meth in 2003, 2007, and 2009? What percentages of teens in neighboring South Dakota reported doing likewise in those years?

3. Despite the Montana Meth Project's successes, what proportion of Montana law enforcement officials believe meth is the state's greatest drug threat and a major contributor to violent crime?

As I conclude more than eight years as U.S. attorney, I want to reflect on Montana's successful attack against methamphetamine. It's also top of mind because, as has recently been reported, *Barron's* magazine cited the Montana Meth Project among the five most effective foundations in the world. In crafting the Montana Meth Project, the Siebel Foundation applied private-sector principles to the structure and execution of a prevention campaign. In this respect, the lessons of the Meth Project are instructive beyond the fight against methamphetamine.

Reducing the Profitability of Drugs by Reducing Demand

For roughly four decades, we have spent substantial state and federal funds on drug enforcement, education and treatment. Investigators and prosecutors target those involved in selling drugs to reduce the supply. Enforcement is essential to disrupt distribution networks by making the cost of doing business (i.e., getting locked up in federal prison) too great. Enforcement also makes drugs less affordable by driving up the cost by reducing supply.

However, even vigorous and well-publicized enforcement operations cannot adequately suppress existing demand because of the grip of addiction. Due to meth's highly addictive nature, demand for treatment outpaces our capacity to provide it.

To reduce drug use, government also allocates funds for prevention through schools and marketing campaigns. Not all education efforts are equally effective. What works is on display with the Montana Meth Project: strategic planning based upon data, implementation based upon lessons learned in the strategic planning and empirical evaluation.

An Effective Campaign Based on Market Research

The Meth Project conducted research and focus groups to guide content of the ads and message delivery. Rather than use public service announcements, the Meth Project paid for spots in prime time. After each wave of ads, they resurveyed Montanans to assess whether the campaign was changing behavior and knowledge.

About those ads. The chief complaint seemed to be that they were too edgy. Perhaps they were. But the Meth Project crew knew their target audience from the survey data.

Did the ads work? By 2009, teen meth use, meth-positive workplace drug tests and meth-related crime all had dropped by significant levels. And Montana's teens became stakeholders through the anti-meth Paint-the-State mural competition and the March Against Meth in Helena.

Other jurisdictions have not been as fortunate. According to the Centers for Disease Control [and Prevention], in 2003, 9.3 percent of Montana teens reported using meth on at least one occasion; South Dakota reported a smaller number (7.4 percent) for the same period. In 2007, two years after the launch of the Meth Project, only 4.6 percent of Montana's teens reported using meth on one or more occasions whereas South Dakota had a higher percentage (5.0 percent). In February 2009, only 3.1 percent of Montana high school students reported ever using methamphetamine and only 1 percent of Montana high school sophomores disclosed past meth use.

The demand for meth skyrocketed in the first half of the decade. In fiscal years 2001 through 2004, an annual average of 105 federal defendants were sentenced for methamphetamine distribution cases brought by my office. Until recently, distribution networks tied to Mexican suppliers continued to penetrate the Montana market at high rates. In 2005, 121 defendants were sentenced for drug offenses, 90 involving methamphetamine distribution. In 2008, 83 of 112 drug defendants were penalized for meth distribution. However, as 2009 draws to a close, only 46 federal defendants have been sentenced for methamphetamine offenses.

Successfully Suppressing Demand

Today [December 2009], the supply of meth is well below pre-Meth Project levels, in large part because demand is way down. The number of teens disclosing use has dropped by two-thirds in the second half of the decade. What changed in this period? The Meth Project made meth use socially unacceptable; now Montanans share awareness of its ills.

The Meth Project works because of the strategic manner in which it was shaped and the frequent testing of its efforts.

Furthermore, Montanans cannot afford to declare victory. Even after big gains against meth, my colleagues in local law enforcement continue to view the drug as a very serious problem. The National Drug Intelligence Center at the Department of Justice reported in March that 10 of 14 law enforcement officials in Montana identified meth as our greatest drug threat and 14 of 14 named meth the drug that contributes most to violent crime.

Most important, today's 7-year-old will not be affected by ads from 2009 when she is in high school. Like it or not, this messaging will need to be reiterated periodically if we hope to protect today's grade-schoolers from the perils of meth in the next decade.

VIEWPOINT

| "The campaign raises awareness among parents but has done little to alter teen drug use."

Anti-Drug Ad Campaigns Don't Work

Wendy Melillo

The following viewpoint was originally published in ADWEEK, a weekly American advertising trade publication, following the release of early reports from a Government Accountability Office (GAO) probe into the effectiveness of the White House Office of National Drug Control Policy's (ONDCP's) anti-drug advertising campaigns. Westat—the research firm that evaluated the program for the GAO—ultimately concluded that "greater exposure to the campaign was associated with weaker anti-drug norms and increases in the perceptions that others use marijuana." The GAO establishes standards for, and evaluates the efficacy and efficiency of, government programs.

As you read, consider the following questions:

1. How much has been spent on evaluating the effectiveness of the ONDCP's anti-drug advertising campaign

since 1998? Is this a significant percentage of the $1 billion that has been spent on the campaign?

2. According to GAO managing director Nancy Kingsbury, what is puzzling about the GAO's response to the Westat evaluation of their anti-drug ad-campaign?

3. According to ONDCP representative Tom Riley, how did adult and teen drug use rates change during the period of this advertising campaign?

A Government Accountability Office probe of the White House's anti-drug media campaign has found that the $1 billion-plus spent on the effort so far has not been effective in reducing teen drug use. The report recommends that Congress limit funding until the Office of National Drug Control Policy "provides credible evidence of a media campaign approach that effectively prevents and curtails youth drug use."

Questions About How to Evaluate the Program

The report comes at a time when Congress is poised to take up the anti-drug media campaign budget [once] it returns from its [2006] recess. The campaign's current budget is $99 million, the lowest since the effort began in 1998. ONDCP has asked for $120 million next year. The Senate agrees with that amount, but the House has recommended $100 million.

The GAO report examined the Westat survey, named after the Rockville, Md., research firm that was awarded the contract in 1998 to evaluate the campaign. Since then, the government has spent $42 million on a survey that has been a constant thorn in ONDCP's side because critics argue that it uses a flawed methodology. The survey has concluded that the campaign raises awareness among parents but has done little to alter teen drug use.

Critics charge that Westat did not start measuring the campaign's effectiveness until nearly 18 months after the launch, so the baseline is off. Westat once reported that the campaign contributed to an increase in marijuana use among teenage girls, a finding that captured media attention. When the campaign changed its target audience and creative [advertising] was directed at 11- to 15-year-olds, Westat continued to measure the previous demo of 9- to 11-year-olds and was unable to measure the new target.

In a five-page response to the GAO report, drug czar John Walters questions the validity of the Westat measurement tool because it seeks to directly prove that advertising caused teens to stop using drugs. "Establishing a causal relationship between exposure and outcomes is something major marketers rarely attempt because it is virtually impossible to do," Walters wrote. "This is one reason why the 'Truth' anti-tobacco advertising campaign, acclaimed as a successful initiative in view of the significant declines we've seen in teen smoking, did not claim to prove a causal relationship between campaign exposure and smoking outcomes, reporting instead that the campaign was associated with substantial declines in youth smoking."

Probe Follows Convictions of Top Officials on Campaign

Nancy Kingsbury, the GAO's managing director of applied research methods, said Walters raised a valid point. "It is a really tough social science question to answer and we understand that," she said. "What puzzles us is that when the [Westat] contract was first put in place, ONDCP got a lot of political capital out of the fact that they had an evaluation. But it's just that it did not come out the way they wanted. I still give them credit for doing it. It is the right thing to do."

Kingsbury said Westat has done work in the past for GAO, but that those contracts were in separate divisions that had nothing to do with its current report. Westat handled a $1.6

Even the Lauded Montana Meth Project Doesn't Work

The Montana Meth Project (MMP) is an organization that launched a large-scale methamphetamine prevention program in Montana in 2005. The central component of the program is a graphic advertising campaign that portrays methamphetamine users as unhygienic, dangerous, untrustworthy, and exploitive. Montana teenagers are exposed to the advertisements three to five times a week. The MMP, media and politicians have portrayed the advertising campaign as a resounding success that has dramatically increased anti-methamphetamine attitudes and reduced drug use in Montana. The program is currently being rolled out across the nation, and is receiving considerable public funding. . . . Claims that the campaign is effective are not supported by data. The campaign has been associated with increases in the acceptability of using methamphetamine and decreases in the perceived danger of using drugs. These and other negative findings have been ignored and misrepresented by the MMP. There is no evidence that reductions in methamphetamine use in Montana are caused by the advertising campaign. On the basis of current evidence, continued public funding and rollout of Montana-style methamphetamine programs is inadvisable.

David M. Erceg-Hurn, "Drugs, Money, & Graphic Ads:
A Critical Review of the Montana Meth Project,"
Prevention Science, *December 2008.*

million contract for GAO from 1997–1999 evaluating Medicare and a $534,000 hospital survey done in 2004–2005.

ONDCP has been in a no-win situation since the GAO probe began, which followed the convictions of two top agency officials for overbilling the government on the campaign. As one observer put it at the time the probe was launched, "If the GAO finds that Westat is a piece of crap, then ONDCP has wasted $42 million. If the report says Westat has somehow found the holy grail of advertising cause and effect, then the campaign is not working by that measure."

ONDCP representative Tom Riley points to independent studies showing that teen drug use has declined by 19 percent. "Everybody who follows this issue acknowledges the campaign's role in those great results," he said. "Evaluation is important to us. The most telling statistic is that adult drug use has not appreciably changed while teen drug use [the target of the campaign] has gone down dramatically. I think that's the definition of successful advertising."

Proponents Argue That There Is No Way to Judge Success

Stephen Pasierb, president and CEO of the Partnership for a Drug-Free America, which coordinates creative [advertising] on the campaign through 40 agencies, said the GAO probe provides no new learning for the campaign. "There is nothing you can do with this study to change the campaign," he said. "There is no learning here because it seeks to prove something you can't prove. The campaign was never meant to be this kind of a silver bullet."

The recent GAO report was prompted by a request from Sen. Richard Shelby, R-Ala., to examine all of the contracts that were part of the media campaign, including ads, public relations and evaluation.

Riley said that what matters in the end is balancing the kind of messages teens hear. "Teens are saturated with pro drug messages from rap music, from movies and from other teens around them," he said. "The campaign is the only national source of anti-drug messages and it is vital to continue funding it."

Periodical Bibliography

The following articles have been selected to supplement the diverse views presented in this chapter.

Lisa A. Brady   "Why We Test Students for Drugs: The Superintendent in a New Jersey Suburb Sees a Compelling Message Being Sent to Her Community, Along with Positive Results," *School Administrator*, January 2008.

David J. Hanson   "Alternatives to the Failed D.A.R.E. (Drug Abuse Resistance Education) Program," October 24, 2009. www2.potsdam.edu.

Junior Scholastic   "Real Questions, Real Answers: Leading Scientists Give Teens the Facts About Drug Abuse," November 9, 2009.

Jennifer Kern   "Whether It's Sex or Drugs, Abstinence-Only Education Simply Doesn't Work," *AlterNet*, September 10, 2008. www.alternet.org.

Damian McNamara   "Early Intervention Urged in Teen Substance Use," *Pediatric News*, September 2007.

Maia Szalavitz   "Economy Killing Abusive Teen Programs," *Mother Jones*, January 30, 2009. http://motherjones.com.

Science World   "The Truth About: 'Rehab' and Drug Addiction: The Reality Is Far from Glamorous," April 6, 2009.

For Further Discussion

Chapter 1

1. In their viewpoint, Mike Linderman and Gary Brozek persuasively argue that all teen drug or alcohol use is abuse. Conversely, Stanton Peele argues that little such drug use constitutes addiction; is it possible to abuse drugs without being an addict? Peele makes clear that many "addicts" do not abuse any substances; can you define the term "drug abuse" without using the word "addiction"?

2. Since the term "pharm party" was first coined in the mid-2000s, the idea that teens gather to randomly take pilfered pills has gained increasing traction in TV dramas and news reports. Based on the arguments presented by Liz Doup and Jack Shafer, do you believe these parties really exist?

Chapter 2

1. Based on the viewpoints you have read and your own personal beliefs, do you believe the drinking age should be lowered, raised, or kept the same? Or should the drinking age be abolished altogether? Why or why not? Some people advocate shifting to a "graduated drinking age," similar to the graduated driver's licenses used in many states; would this work better than the current policies governing alcohol sale, possession, and consumption?

2. Considering the many negative health impacts associated with alcohol use—even among those who can do so legally—why is it legal at all? If you believe the failure of Prohibition proves that Americans demand the right to drink, do you likewise feel that society should repeal laws prohibiting the possession and use of all drugs?

Chapter 3

1. In light of what you learned in the second viewpoint, have your opinions on teen drinking (and the drinking age) changed?

2. Based on what you have read in this chapter, do you believe that drug use *causes* teens to behave in anti-social ways, or that teens with anti-social tendencies tend to gravitate toward using drugs? Is it possible to determine which is the case? Do the two cases require two different solutions, or can both be addressed with a single policy?

Chapter 4

1. Do Maia Szalavitz and Benedict Carey agree or disagree as to what constitutes the most (or possibly only) useful treatment for rehabilitating teen drug abusers?

2. In his viewpoint, David J. Hanson argues that the DARE program has little impact on teen drug use, and can even increase adolescents' self-identified perception that drug use (including tobacco) is common, acceptable behavior. Wendy Melillo likewise reported that the Government Accountability Office (GAO) found that government-funded anti-drug advertisements had little impact on teen behavior, and may even encourage drug use. In light of everything you've read in this chapter, how should the government allocate funds in order to best curb teen drug abuse?

Organizations to Contact

The editors have compiled the following list of organizations concerned with the issues debated in this book. The descriptions are derived from materials provided by the organizations. All have publications or information available for interested readers. The list was compiled on the date of publication of the present volume; the information provided here may change. Be aware that many organizations take several weeks or longer to respond to inquiries, so allow as much time as possible.

Alcoholics Anonymous (AA)
PO Box 459, New York, NY   10163
(212) 870-3400
Web site: www.aa.org

Alcoholics Anonymous sponsors informal groups of men and women who work together to support each other in staying sober and helping others to recover from alcoholism. The organization was founded in the 1940s by Bill Wilson and Bob Smith, the originators of the twelve-step program for reaching sobriety. The AA Web site offers information on the organization, its methods, and how to find local AA meetings.

American Civil Liberties Union (ACLU)
125 Broad Street, 18th Floor, New York, NY   10004-2400
(212) 549-2500
e-mail: aclu@aclu.org
Web site: www.aclu.org

The American Civil Liberties Union is dedicated to preserving freedoms of expression and religious practice, and rights to privacy, due process, and equal protection under the law. It provides free legal services to those whose rights have been violated. The ACLU Web site offers an array of policy statements, pamphlets, and fact sheets on civil rights issues, including *Making Sense of Student Drug Testing: Why Educators Are Saying No* and *ACLU Fact Sheet: Social Science Research on Adolescent Drug Use and School Involvement.*

The Cool Spot

National Institute on Alcohol Abuse and Alcoholism
Bethesda, MD   20892-9304
Web site: www.thecoolspot.gov

The *Cool Spot* Web site is maintained by the National Institute on Alcohol Abuse and Alcoholism (NIAAA). This Web site offers materials on alcohol, resisting peer pressure, and finding help for alcohol addiction that are geared toward young teens (ages eleven to thirteen years). This literature draws on the research-based curriculum developed at the University of Michigan for the large-scale Alcohol Misuse Prevention Study (AMPS) sponsored by NIAAA.

Choose Responsibility

10 E Street SE, Washington, DC   20003
(202) 543-8760
e-mail: info@chooseresponsibility.org
Web site: www.chooseresponsibility.org

Choose Responsibility is a nonprofit organization dedicated to increasing public awareness of the hazards associated with reckless drinking among young adults (especially college students), and to promote lowering the minimum drinking age. The founder and director of Choose Responsibility, John McCardell Jr. (president emeritus of Vermont's Middlebury College), also drafted the "Amethyst Initiative" (www.amethyst initiative.org), which urges a reconsideration of current age restrictions on alcohol purchase and possession. The Amethyst Initiative has been signed by more than 100 college and university presidents across the United States.

Monitoring the Future
University of Michigan, Ann Arbor, MI 48109
(734) 764-7260
Web site: www.monitoringthefuture.org

Since 1975 the University of Michigan has conducted its annual Monitoring the Future survey, which tracks adolescent drug use patterns and attitudes. Monitoring the Future anonymously surveys 50,000 eighth-, tenth-, and twelfth-graders each year, and compiles responses into a report that is released to the public (as is the data it is based on) and made available on its Web site.

Mothers Against Drunk Driving (MADD)
511 E. John Carpenter Freeway, Suite 700, Irving, TX 75062
(800) GET-MADD (438-6233)
Web site: www.madd.org

Founded in 1980, Mothers Against Drunk Driving has established missions to stop drunk driving, support the victims of drunk driving, and prevent underage drinking. MADD seeks to do so through public education, through lobbying for stricter laws governing alcohol sale and possession, and through harsher punishment for individuals who drive while intoxicated. The MADD Web site hosts a wide variety of fact sheets, educational materials, and action plans.

Narcotics Anonymous
PO Box 9999, Van Nuys, CA 91409
(818) 773-9999
Web site: www.na.org

Narcotics Anonymous (NA) is an organization similar to Alcoholics Anonymous in its structure and aims, and it grew out of AA in the 1950s. Based on a similar twelve-step program, NA sponsors many local chapters composed of men and women who support each other in overcoming drug addiction and avoiding further drug use. The NA Web site offers online versions of NA literature, self-help texts, and a search engine for finding local chapters.

National Center on Substance Abuse at Columbia University (CASA)

633 Third Ave., 19th Floor, New York, NY   10017-6706
(212) 841-5200
Web site: www.casacolumbia.org

Joseph A. Califano Jr. established CASA (the Center on Addiction and Substance Abuse, later renamed the National Center on Substance Abuse at Columbia University) in 1992. A former United States Secretary of Health, Education, and Welfare, Califano founded CASA to educate Americans about the economic and social costs of drug abuse, and to help remove the stigma associated with substance abuse and dependence. The CASA Web site hosts a wide variety of downloadable reports, press releases, and news items.

The National Institute on Drug Abuse (NIDA)

The National Institutes of Health, Bethesda, MD   20892-9561
(301) 443-1124
e-mail: information@nida.nih.gov
Web site: http://www.drugabuse.gov

The National Institute on Drug Abuse is a part of the United States National Institutes of Health, which sponsors research into a wide range of health-related topics. NIDA focuses on rigorous scientific research into drug abuse and distributing such findings. The Web site "NIDA for Teens" (www.teens.drugabuse.gov) provides information about drugs and addiction geared toward teenagers.

National Organization for the Reform of Marijuana Laws (NORML)

1600 K Street NW, Suite 501, Washington, DC   20006-2832
(202) 483-5500
e-mail: norml@norml.org
Web site: www.norml.org

The National Organization for the Reform of Marijuana Laws is a nonprofit organization dedicated to the repeal of cannabis prohibition in the United States. NORML seeks to change attitudes toward marijuana through public education campaigns, through lobbying for changes in state and federal law, and by offering legal services to individuals being prosecuted for cannabis-related crimes. Its Web site provides many articles, reports, and other resources on the social, legal, and economic repercussions of current marijuana policy.

The Partnership for a Drug-Free America
405 Lexington Ave., Suite 1601, New York, NY 10174
(212) 922-1560
Web site: www.drugfree.org

The Partnership for a Drug-Free America was founded in 1986 as a project of the American Association of Advertising Agencies intended to use existing marketing techniques to "unsell" drugs. Today the group "unites parents, renowned scientists and communications professionals to help families raise healthy children" through the wide deployment of public education programs and multimedia campaigns, all of which are available at its Web site.

Book Bibliography

Judith Aldridge   *Illegal Leisure Revisited: Changing Patterns of Alcohol and Drug Use in Adolescents and Young Adults.* New York: Routledge, 2010.

David Aretha   *On the Rocks: Teens and Alcohol.* Danbury, CT: Children's Press, 2007.

Chris Beckman   *Clean: A New Generation in Recovery Speaks Out.* Center City, MN: Hazelden, 2005.

Sterling R. Braswell   *American Meth: A History of the Methamphetamine Epidemic in America.* Bloomington, IN: iUniverse, 2006.

Marcus Brotherton   *Buzz: A Graphic Reality Check for Teens Dealing with Drugs and Alcohol.* Colorado Springs: Multnomah Books, 2006.

Jeffrey Butts and John Roman   *Juvenile Drug Courts and Teen Substance Abuse.* Washington, DC: Urban Institute Press, 2004.

T. Suzanne Eller   *Real Teens, Real Stories, Real Life.* Colorado Springs: RiverOak, 2002.

Joan Esherick   *Dying for Acceptance: A Teen's Guide to Drug- and Alcohol-Related Health Issues.* Broomall, PA: Mason Crest Publishers, 2004.

Jack Gantos   *Hole in My Life.* New York: Farrar, Straus and Giroux, 2004.

Corbin G. Keech and Charles W. Fairchild — *Dude, What Are My Rights? The Self-Help Legal Survival Guide for Ages 18–25.* Kansas City: Keechild Enterprises, 2004.

KidsPeace — *I've Got This Friend Who: Advice for Teens and Their Friends on Alcohol, Drugs, Eating Disorders, Risky Behavior and More.* Center City, MN: Hazelden, 2007.

Rebecca Janes — *Generation RX: Kids on Pills—A Parent's Guide.* Denver: Outskirts Press, 2009.

Sandra Augustyn Lawton — *Drug Information for Teens: Health Tips About the Physical and Mental Effects of Substance Abuse.* Detroit: Omnigraphics, 2006.

Nicholas R. Lessa and Sara Dulaney Gilbert — *Living with Alcoholism and Drug Addiction.* New York: Checkmark Books, 2009.

Jessi Lohman — *The Truth About Drugs and Teens: An Informed Perspective.* Bloomington, IN: AuthorHouse, 2005.

Jonas Pomere — *Frequently Asked Questions About Drug Testing.* New York: Rosen Publishing Group, 2007.

Nick Reding — *Methland: The Death and Life of an American Small Town.* New York: Bloomsbury USA, 2009.

James Salant — *Leaving Dirty Jersey: A Crystal Meth Memoir.* New York: Simon Spotlight Entertainment, 2008.

Katie John Sharp   *Teenagers and Tobacco: Nicotine and the Adolescent Brain.* Philadelphia: Mason Crest Publishers, 2008.

Lonny Shavelson   *Hooked: Five Addicts Challenge Our Misguided Drug Rehab System.* New York: The New Press, 2002.

Nic Sheff   *Tweak: Growing Up on Methamphetamines.* New York: Atheneum, 2009.

Virginia Vitzthum, Laura Longhine, and Keith Hefner   *The High That Couldn't Last: Teens and Drugs, From Experimentation to Addiction.* New York: Youth Communication, 2010.

Stephen Wallace   *Reality Gap: Alcohol, Drugs, and Sex—What Parents Don't Know and Teens Aren't Telling.* New York: Union Square Press, 2008.

Index

A

Addiction Proof Your Child: A Realistic Approach to Preventing Drug, Alcohol, and Other Dependencies (Peele), 33–39

Addictions
  causes of, 35–36
  detraction from living with, 37–38
  disagreements about nature of, 36
  expanded definition of, 37
  normal obsession vs., 38–39
  range/types of, 36–37

Advisory Panel on the Misuse of Drugs (Great Britain), 122

Age at Drinking Onset and Alcohol Dependence (Hingson, Heeren, Winter), 111

Age at first drink (AFD), 109–110, 111–112

Age 21 drinking age policy
  death prevented by, 104
  enforcement support for, 106–106
  public/scientific support for, 104–105
  traffic safety/health benefits of, 102–103
  See also Underage drinking

Agrawal, Arpana, 108–110, 112–113

Alcohol and Drug Abuse Institute (University of Washington), 64

Alcohol dependence (AD), 109–110, 112–113

Alcohol use
  for being "grown up," 29–30
  as bonding behavior, 23–25
  by college students, 22, 101, 106
  drug use compared with, 30–32
  dysfunctional needs satisfied by, 22–23
  for excusing mistakes, 28
  genetic basis for, 109–110, 112
  high school senior trends, 15
  MADD/SADD programs, 15–16
  male/female percentages, 22
  moderate home drinking, 84–87
  negatives of, 28–29
  NSDUH survey on, 21–22
  religion and, 144
  sex and, 141
  Surgeon General's report, 22–23
  twelve year olds/eighteen year olds, 22
  university studies of, 82–83
  See also Drinking age; National Institute of Alcoholism and Alcohol Abuse

American Academy of Child and Adolescent Psychiatry, 138

American Civil Liberties Union (ACLU), 158, 160

American Drug and Alcohol Survey (Rocky Mountain Behavioral Science Institute), 170

American Journal of Diseases of Children, 62

223